AF266853

THE COMPASS BROKE, I KEPT WALKING

*A Story of Collapse, Clarity,
and the Courage to Continue*

William B. Seymour

THE COMPASS BROKE, I KEPT WALKING
A STORY OF COLLAPSE, CLARITY, AND THE COURAGE TO CONTINUE
Written by Bill Seymour

Paperback ISBN: 978-1-967587-54-4
eBook ISBN: 978-1-967587-55-1

This publication is designed to provide accurate and authoritative information regarding the subject matter covered. It is sold with the understanding that the publisher is not engaged in rendering legal, accounting, or other professional services. If you require legal advice or other expert assistance, you should seek the services of a competent professional.

Design and cover art by Peaceful Profits.

DISCLAIMER: The information contained in this book is provided for educational purposes only and should not be construed as legal, financial, tax, or investment advice. Readers are strongly encouraged to consult with a qualified and licensed professional who can provide advice tailored to their individual circumstances. Laws, regulations, and financial practices vary across countries, states, and regions. Market conditions, returns, and outcomes will differ over time and cannot be guaranteed. While every effort has been made to provide accurate and timely information at the time of writing, we make no representations or warranties regarding completeness, accuracy, or applicability. We are not making any official legal or financial recommendations. The examples, figures, and principles presented herein are for illustrative and educational purposes only. Any decisions you make are solely your responsibility.

Dedication

*To everyone I've had the privilege of crossing paths with—
whether for a moment or a season—thank you. Your presence,
however brief or lasting, has shaped the contours of my
journey. May your steps be guided by truth, and may your
path—however winding—lead you to the clarity and courage
you were always meant to find.*

Before you begin—know this:

I don't have all the answers. Just a pile of scars.
The first time I lost everything, I didn't cry—I took notes.
Found out, we don't break all at once.

We fracture in places no one sees.
And every scar I carry has a story.

This is the story I finally chose to tell.

Contents

Foreword: A Quiet Rebellion

I don't have all the answers. But I do have stories, scars, and the stubborn will to keep showing up.

I didn't write this book to teach you how to live.

I wrote it because I've lived long enough to know most of the rules we're handed don't fit. They sound good in speeches. They look polished in books. But they rarely survive the mess of real life—heartbreaks, detours, and the quiet mornings when you wonder what it's all for.

I've been a cop. A soldier. A business owner. A husband. A father.

I've been a man who's loved, lost, and learned to love again. I've built things. Broken things. Rebuilt myself more than once. And through it all, I've come to believe that the most important truths aren't shouted. They whisper. They unfold in the margins—like ink bleeding through the edges of a page you thought was blank.

So, if you're here looking for steps, formulas, or guarantees in these pages—you won't find them. What you will find are Billisms: reflections, reminders, and quiet rebellions against the noise. They're not commandments. They're observations. They're the kind of truths that sit with you, not lecture you.

Some are about kindness. Some about failure. Some about golf balls that refuse to listen. But all of them come from a place of lived experience. From a man who's still learning, still evolving, and still curious about what the next page holds.

If something here speaks to you, stay awhile. If it doesn't, that's okay too. This book isn't here to lead. It's here to walk beside you—especially when the road disappears. It's here to remind you that your journey, with all its missteps and miracles, is already enough.

The First Time I Questioned the Frame

I t doesn't begin with an answer. It begins with the whisper of a question.

"Did it all really happen?"

What I saw. What I endured. What I became.

I was there for every moment—yet some days, my own memories feel borrowed. Like a myth someone else lived, and I got stuck with the scars. Some days, the memories roar back—treacherous, electric, surreal. Other days, they flicker like echoes from a life I almost recognize.

Maybe you've felt it too. That strange dissonance between who you are and what the world allows you to be. Maybe your mask fits so well that even the mirror stopped asking who you are. You wear the mask not to deceive, but to defend. Not a lie, but a shield. Armor against a world that never asked who you truly are.

If that's your truth, then hear this:

You can reinvent yourself at any time.

I've ripped the mask from my own face. Stripped away the layers that once protected me, and unearthed the freedom of living as I truly am. I was born into nothing. No script. No pedigree. Just hunger. Just questions. And an obsession with decoding what it means to live fully—not perfectly.

Over the decades, I've carved a life from raw experience and relentless perseverance. I've been redirected more times than I can count. Built myself up from nothing, amassed millions, lost everything, and then rebuilt it all once more. Triumph. Collapse. Victory. Setback. Again, and again, and again.

That cycle? It became my rhythm.

The many crashes—in business, in relationships, in the crumbling foundations of what I thought I knew—became another chance to rise.

Today, I've traveled the world and built something lasting from scratch, and I am successful. Not because of money or accolades, but because I wake up grateful. Because I no longer hide from the scars, and because I know what it means to own my truth and still smile at the sunrise.

This book isn't a manual. It's a mirror. A compass. A path through the wreckage toward becoming something whole.

These lived-in stories of redirection and reinvention I now offer to you. Not as answers, but as invitations to reflect and rewrite yourself in real time—to reclaim your narrative before it claims you.

For this reason, every chapter ends with a quiet reflection, woven like threads that stitch meaning into each story. A single page of hard-earned wisdom, a grounding philosophy, shared with no agenda but this:

To invite your own reflection.

So, as you hold this book in your hands, know this—I'm not here to impress.

I'm here to remind you of the kind of clarity that only appears once you've stopped chasing someone else's version of peace. I'm here to show you that you are not done. You are not broken. You are simply beginning again.

Just as I have done countless times.

With our broken compasses, let us walk these roads together. So you, too, may make peace with your scars, find your true north, and wake each day to smile at the sunrise that greets you.

Let's begin.

Forward. Together.

"WHAT IT IS, IS WHAT IT IS."

– William (Bill) Seymour

Act One

Foundations in Fire

Chapter One
Born Into the Noise

Welfare Walls & Hustle Heart

I was born into noise—of hunger, of anger, of survival. Before I knew what dreams were, I knew what survival felt like.

I grew up in a cramped railroad apartment with my two younger brothers, two older sisters, our mother, and a few uninvited tenants: mice and roaches crammed inside with us. My father had left months earlier, chasing a new life in Florida—leaving us behind in Brooklyn, struggling to keep afloat. Our apartment was a long, narrow, open space—six small, dimly lit rooms lined up one after another, connected through doorless entryways like the carriages of a classic steam train.

It sat above a music store, one in a row of shops crowned with small apartments. That was Flatbush Ave, Brooklyn—raw, crowded, real. Just a fragile refuge for broken families, held together by welfare checks and a $90 per month rent that barely kept our family of six under one roof.

I remember the mice—darting across the floor, too fast for my eyes to catch.

In the beginning, my sisters used to shriek loudly in fear as the skittering little feet of the mice scampered across our own bare feet. And the roaches—always there, always moving. But I didn't scream. I didn't run. I just stepped over them like they lived there, too. Because that's just how it was; they were residents in that small apartment just as much as we were.

I never wanted to kill the mice. I'd catch them and cart them outside in a worn brown cardboard box and let them loose in the long brown grass of an empty lot a few blocks away.

I didn't extend the same kindness to the roaches.

I remember the ceiling of that railroad apartment, leaking from flooding, from the maintenance neglect of the neighbors above. The ceiling shook viciously as the couple upstairs screamed at each other, their voices crashing through the thin walls. Sometimes, I wondered if the plaster of the ceiling would crack open—their rage tumbling down on us.

Most of all, I remember the beads. Big boxes of plastic beads— white, opaque, pink, blue, and green—delivered like clockwork. They filled our cramped little kitchen and small living room, and all of us—five kids plus Mom—sat shoulder to shoulder, stringing them together, turning beads into necklaces, turning necklaces into money. Thirty bucks a box—that's what my mother earned from our long hours of finger-numbing work.

Four boxes, or $120 a month. That was all we had to live on. Well, that plus one small welfare check that came in the last week of the month—the week that we all waited impatiently for the mail to arrive.

It wasn't enough. Not even close. How we survived is a miracle.

I hated those beads. I hated how our whole world was wrapped around them, how they gave us just enough scraps to survive. But nothing more. And I hated knowing, even at 7 years old, that I wanted more than this. I wasn't going to stay in this tiny, dark apartment, making cheap necklaces for the rest of my life.

It became my life's mission: becoming more. A through line that has guided every major decision I've made in my life.

Even at 7, I was already watching, already learning, already plotting my escape.

Not from my family. From the frame I was born into. I didn't know what more looked like—I just knew it wasn't beads. It wasn't roaches. It wasn't waiting for the mail like it carried oxygen. More was freedom. Though I wouldn't know how to name it until much later.

After all, what does a 7-year-old know about dreams? Not much. But I knew silence. I knew hunger. And I knew there was something out there, bigger than the noise I'd been born into.

Even as a child, I understood—nobody but me could decide.

At school, I kept my eyes open and kept my hands ready for opportunity. Every day, I earned a couple of coins. I picked up empty bottles off the street and returned them for a few cents. I asked old ladies if I could carry their packages for tips. I shoveled snow in the winter. I saved every penny I got from my aunts and uncles—small, financial gifts from birthdays, Christmas, my church confirmation, and my elementary school graduation. Every coin was capital, every gift a seed. So I collected each penny like it was forged from pure gold. I was determined to make something of myself and my life.

Down the block from our home was a shoe repair shop—one I went to a lot, since my own shoes were falling apart. I shoved cardboard inside them just to keep my feet off the pavement.

Every time I was there, I watched. I watched how the man moved, how customers lined up and let him work his magic. Under his hands, shoes transformed—dull leather turned sleek, shining, proud.

I could do that too. I could do it *better.*

My eyes honed in on the little metal footstool he had, the one his customers placed their feet upon while he shined their shoes. I wondered how I could get one for myself. So, I asked.

The shoeshiner looked at me—really looked at me—and I think he saw something in my eyes, heard something in my voice that told him I meant business. That told him I wasn't just some kid playing pretend.

He didn't laugh. He didn't tell me no. Instead, he nodded, disappeared into the back, and came out with an old footstool, one just like his.

"Here," he said, handing it over. "Go make something of it, kid."

I nodded, clutching the stool like a scepter. Destiny doesn't always come with fireworks. Sometimes, it's a quiet transfer of belief.

And that, that was all I needed.

At home, I found an old ammo box, one of the few things my dad had left behind from his time as a Marine who served in World War II. I took the small metal footstool I'd gotten from the shoeshiner and screwed it right on top of that wooden ammo box to make a platform for people to more comfortably rest their feet upon. Then I took the money I had saved and went back to the shoe repair guy, buying everything I'd need— buffing rags, jars of polish, and shoelaces. Three different colors of laces, to be precise, and three different colors of polish: black, brown, and clear.

Just like that, I had a business.

Out on the street, right outside our apartment, I yelled as loud as I could—"SHOESHINE! SHOESHINE!"—until someone stopped and let me work on their shoes.

I made sure I wasn't just good. I made sure I was the *best*. Let me be clear—I'm not a perfectionist. But I've also never taken a test aiming to get a 93. My personality has always been to try for a 100%, and then be happy with any result, so long as I tried my best.

And then be determined to improve.

I always take pride in anything I do, and it has set me apart time and time again. In fact, within a few weeks, people started telling me—"Bill, your shoeshine is top-notch," and they meant it.

I wrapped their crisp white socks in a cloth before I polished their shoes, so they wouldn't get dirty. I'd offer to change their laces for another dime if I noticed they were frayed. I spritzed water on their shoes to give them an extra gleam—I had watched the shoe guy do that. So I did it too. A technique learned by observing intently, which made their leather shoes look brand-new.

At first, I was just some kid on the corner with a stool and a polish rag. Before long, I had regulars. I wasn't just hustling anymore—I was earning respect. A reputation. A line of people waiting just for me.

And then came Barney.

Work is an Art

Barney wasn't just one of my best customers. He was a spark. The impetus of something more.

A little old Italian guy with sun-worn skin and an accent thick as tomato paste. He owned Crystal Gardens, the fruit market down the block. One day, while I was shining his loafers, he looked at me intentionally, "Hey kid, did you ever think about doing something besides shining shoes?"

Yes, I told him.

I was already delivering newspapers every morning before school. I went door-to-door a few months back, ringing the bells of every house, asking if they wanted a newspaper delivered straight to their stoop each morning. I recruited every customer myself, just like I did with my shoeshine business. And every morning, I delivered the rolled-up newspapers on my bike at 6:30 am before school.

I had no time to do anything else, not with school and the jobs I was already doing. I told Barney as much. But he insisted.

"Come to my store," he said. "Help me set up the fruit stand. I'll pay you well for it."

I figured it didn't hurt to go see it. I wasn't one to turn down an opportunity, after all. And I was always a polite kid; I didn't want to be rude. I also didn't want to lose him as a steady customer.

So the next morning, I went. I remember it was a Saturday. I saw how he threw the fruit onto the shelves—just dumped them on the wooden stands outside the store, no care, no thought—actually bruising the fruit he was trying to sell.

I didn't know if fruit had feelings. But I knew that if it looked battered, people walked past. If it shined, they stopped. I also knew I could do it better. So on top of everything else, I agreed to take on the job at Barney's fruit store.

My future shifted, quietly at first but unmistakably. If I had to name the spark that lit the road ahead—it was him. Barney. If there was a moment that rewrote the terms of my path, a moment that turned inertia into ignition—it was this.

I lined up the apples, one by one, and made sure every piece of fruit sat neat, clean, and perfect. The apples came wrapped in soft white paper. I stripped them down and polished them—just like I did with the shoes.

When I finished, the fruit stand didn't look like a market shelf—it looked like art.

It caught eyes. Made people stop. Made them want to buy. And buy more. Lots more.

Barney and his partner, Vinny, took notice. They knew I wasn't just another kid—I was a kid who was making them more money.

So I got a promotion. Not just setting up fruit, but bagging groceries and taking care of customers, at only 7 years old. Running the cash register and delivering orders straight to customers' homes by age 8. Every Saturday, after we closed up, Barney let me fill two giant shopping bags with anything I wanted. It was part of my pay.

But I got savvy.

During the week, when he asked if I wanted anything, I'd just say, "Yeah, can I take a few pounds of potatoes?"

I didn't touch the fruit. Didn't touch the good stuff, because I knew that potatoes didn't count toward my Saturday perk.

All week, my family ate potatoes. But on Saturday, I filled two grocery bags with fresh, colorful, mouthwatering fruit and vegetables—the kind of stuff we'd barely tasted before.

We ate salads. Big, bright, beautiful salads.

My sisters made these elaborate salads every night—so colorful they looked like dessert. And just like dessert, we always ate salad last. There was always room for salad. I was a growing young boy. I ate a lot.

We ate better. We lived better.

My first brushes with poverty and hardship came so young, I scarcely have memory of my first encounter. But by 8 years old, with a belly full of salad and potatoes, and a mind committed to moving me forward, I drowned out the noise I'd been born into. My circumstances did not define me.

They *shaped* me.

Word spread fast. People talked about the neighborhood kid who came from nothing, but had an incomparable work ethic. By 9 years old, I was making real money, yes, but I was just getting started.

I thought I had hustled as hard as a kid could hustle. But I was wrong. The real turning point was just ahead—and it would change everything.

***A Quiet Reflection:** There were many times I felt more caretaker than child—managing moods, tiptoeing around landmines. These circumstances could have created love and empathy, or they could have festered anger and resentment.*

The choice was always there. But it was a choice.

Children need love and guidance, and without it, I might have chosen anger. Instead, I carried instinct. I trusted it more than advice—and still do.

I was loved by my mother, sisters, and brothers. I was mentored by men who saw my instinct and applauded it, encouraging it to grow into a fine-tuned weapon I could wield against life's injustices.

And so, I began to build.

The mirror told me who I was supposed to be. The cracks in that mirror told me who I really was. Not someone defined by circumstance, but someone who was determined to be the difference.

For The Reader: *This difference is not something to be feared. If something in your mind or body urges you toward a different path—listen. Listen to your own wisdom, your internal compass, and take the road less-traveled. Don't be afraid, for even whispers can lead revolutions.*

Be somebody, no matter what you were given.

Be somebody more.

Do something with the more you become—and make a difference.

Don't just live. Ignite.

Be a thinker. Say to yourself: " How do I change this?" That is what I have done throughout my life from the young age of 7, and it has never failed me to this day of writing at age 75.

You already know how to become something more. The answer isn't out there—it's in you.

Don't search for proof in others. *Don't seek it outside of yourself; find it within and call it forth.* ***Fan it like a flame.***

And then—burn bright enough to light the way for someone else.

The Day I Began to Trust my Own Mind

"In a world that often demands noise and affirmation, I was learning to navigate by a different compass. Trusting myself wasn't loud—it was steady."

–Bill

A Boy Carrying a Man's Load

Alan owned Clarendon Laboratories—a prominent clinical laboratory and surgical supply company. He was a tall, lanky man always dressed in a sharp suit and tie. At the time, I wouldn't say I knew Alan well, but I certainly knew of him. He would cross the street to buy fruit regularly, and I'd caught him watching me work, more than a time or two.

Soon enough, Alan and Barney started to talk about me every time Alan was in the shop. Their not-so-hushed conversation began. "I want the kid to come work for me. I could teach him a lot," Alan said.

"Yeah, he's good; he's real smart," Barney responded in his thick Italian accent. My young ears eavesdropped, latching onto every word, itching to be brought into the fray.

One day, Alan crossed the street and offered me a job. "Bill, I've noticed the great work you do here, and I want you to come work for me over at the lab. There's real promise for growth, and I think you'd learn a lot."

Barney strode over and gently tousled my hair in agreement with Alan's offer. "I really think you should go over there, kid. It's an opportunity you can't pass up, and our little shop will get along just fine."

I trusted my instinct that told me to go, and I nodded my head in agreement.

Within weeks, I'd trained my replacement for the fruit store, a stout neighborhood kid, taller and older than me. When training was complete, I crossed the street in my dusty and worn shoes and stepped over the threshold into Alan's pristine laboratory for the first time. It was the opposite of the fruit and vegetable store in every way. Organic fruit, grown from the ground, replaced by sterile metal lab equipment, crafted by man. I was more than impressed by what awaited me inside that lab, but I also didn't feel like I belonged. Immediately, my knees shook. My hands went clammy. My nerves hijacked my steady mind.

The fear was short-lived. No, this pristine lab full of brilliant minds was not beyond me. It was just another challenge. And I loved a challenge.

This marked the third time that I had been given a chance to move my life forward, simply because of how I showed up with the dedication and pride I put into my work. First, with the shoeshiner, then Barney, and now with Alan. These were just the first times in my life that I can recall how much people take notice when you show up fully for everything you do, no matter how big or small the task.

They Asked for Bill

I did all kinds of things at Alan's renowned laboratory. When I was 10, I cleaned out the glass test tubes and beakers, mopped the floors, and wiped down the lab equipment. Then I was trained to do more.

Med, a technologist, quickly took me under his wing. Med was destined for big things, extremely smart, focused, and generous with his knowledge. First, he taught me how to do a urine analysis, measuring and mixing different solutions and chemicals. Then, along with the lab's manager of sorts—a friendly doctor and chiropractor named Dr. Candy—Med taught me hematology (the study of blood), blood disorders, and then chemistry. Soon, I traded scrubbing floors for looking under the microscope and analyzing cultures.

A few years after I started, Alan purchased an SMA-12 Diagnostic Machine for the lab. At the time, it was one of the most sophisticated blood analysis machines on the market because it could run up to 12 tests at once. It cost him a whopping $2 million for us to have at *our* lab.

When the SMA-12 tech came to train Med, he insisted I stay by his side the whole time. "Bill, I want you to learn everything. *Everything* that he's going to teach me—it's for you too. " I nodded eagerly, absorbing every detail.

From that day forward, when Med would use the machine, I watched him and *learned*—my eyes wide with curiosity, my brain whirring with the practical knowledge.

A few more years passed, and Med moved on from the lab when he landed a big job in a very famous hospital in Manhattan. This meant that *I* was the guy left to work the SMA-12 machine. I would be the one to teach others, fully grown men and women, how to use it. I remember these two college grads, right out of Brooklyn College with their shiny new degrees in chemistry still warm in their hands, who came to work at Clarendon Laboratories as the company grew. At this point, I'd just started high school. Yet, I was the one they turned to for advice. *I was training them.* Why?

They had no on-the-job training. I had endless hours of it.

I loved working at that lab. I was good at it. I took great pride in my work. When drawing blood, I could feel the vein pulsing under the tip of my finger. I was able to get the needle in quickly and painlessly. Clients who came in to get their blood drawn would say to me, "Wow, I didn't feel a thing." I'd smile and say, "Were you supposed to?"

Soon enough, I had quite a reputation. Steady, regular customers started asking for me directly when they came in for a blood draw: "The kid, I want the kid to do it."

Alan kept giving me more and more responsibilities—and more pay. By 16, I was making $295 per week plus benefits with three weeks of vacation as an (almost) full-time laboratory technologist. Now, this was in 1966, so that's the equivalent of about $2,900 per week or $150,000 per year today. What can I say? I'd come a long way from that $30 box of beads, and I didn't really see the point of passing up real hard-earned money for finishing high school—which taught me far less than my lived experience and my tenacity had.

Both of which had gotten me to this point in my life.

So I started skipping my classes. In fact, I missed school far more often than I went. Alan often would admonish me: "Go to school, Bill. You're smart, but you still need a formal education. Don't miss out on getting a degree. Life respects effort," he said. "But it also rewards credentials. Don't forget both matter."

But I was still just 17. And 17 is when you mess things up—not always for the thrill, sometimes just out of fear. We all make choices that shape or shake us. Some teach. Some don't. But the chance to choose better once you know better—it's always there, quiet and waiting. You just have to reach for it.

The Good, The Bad, and The Ugly

Skipping school was just the tip of the iceberg. It didn't take long before I dropped out entirely, got my GED, and moved on from the constraints of high school. I didn't feel like I needed it to succeed. I already had a taste for success. Success that I didn't find in a textbook.

It was the 1960s. Everybody was doing drugs, and the rise of counterculture, like the hippie movement, meant that drugs were in high demand. If you asked me today why school took a back seat, I'd give you three reasons: drugs, women, and making money. I won't say I wasn't foolish at the time. But that's my honest answer.

Gone were the shoeshine days of my childhood. As I was approaching 18, I had my salary at the lab, and I had a nice little side hustle as well. I was taking drugs, and I was selling them too.

Yes, I worked for people. But I was a born entrepreneur.

I sold pot and pot only. Friends of mine sold pot too; *everyone was doing it.* Some friends started doing harder drugs. But I had zero interest in the hard stuff.

Zero!

How we sold, though, was what set us apart. Down the block from the lab was a drugstore. It had a big flashing neon sign that said "DRUGS." We sold pot underneath that sign, laughing at the irony of it.

I used my mind here too—everything I'd learned from Barney and Vinny at the fruit stand, and from Alan and Med at the lab. I used it all. I was smart in this little side business of mine. I never carried anything. I would just tell people where I hid the drugs. It was foolproof.

There were many times the cops would conduct raids in my neighborhood, pulling up on guys on street corners and busting their operation. But I never got caught. Never got arrested. I was smart. I can't say the same for all of my friends; they didn't do what I did. And most of them got caught because of it.

During this time, I'd go out to clubs every Thursday, Friday, Saturday, and Sunday night, dancing, sweating, and having a ball. I loved to dance. It was one of the best ways I knew to meet girls. I'd go out with my cousin, Johnny, who was two days younger than me; we were as close as brothers.

Like clockwork, we'd round up our friends and meet every weekend at our favorite spots like a discotheque called The Cheetah in NYC. It was modern and psychedelic and one of the best around. We also loved the Electric Circus in Manhattan, Town House in Brooklyn, and of course, Tempo City Dance Club. If you lived in New York during the '60s, you knew these places. Everybody did.

Still, even in the thick of that high-octane rhythm—working the lab by day, selling by night, and dancing through the weekends—there were quiet moments when it all felt like a hustle built on borrowed time. I remember standing under the DRUGS sign one night, thinking about my friends who got pulled off corners while I somehow skated by.

That irony wasn't always funny. Sometimes, it felt like a warning.

There were nights when I came back from Tempo City, still wired from dancing. I'd sit alone in my room staring at the ceiling, wondering if I was building something or just outrunning everything. The money was good. The girls were beautiful. But I started to notice how quickly good things faded, how easy it was to lose control of what you thought you had handled.

Johnny and I would joke about being too smart to get caught. But deep down, I wasn't cocky—I was calculating. I had watched friends fall not because they weren't smart, but because they didn't see what was coming. I swore I would. And that promise to myself?

It started to feel heavier by the day.

I remember one night at Tempo City—Donna Summer was playing. The bass shook the walls—heavy and hypnotic. But in the corner, two guys whispered about burning their draft cards.

For the first time, the music couldn't drown out my thoughts. The Vietnam War was here, and I couldn't outrun it.

The street smarts, the charm, the hustle—they got me this far. But the draft, the silence, and something deeper were waiting. And they wouldn't wait quietly.

Serving Without Surrendering

War was looming. The reality of the Vietnam War was easy to brush aside when our heads were cloudy with drugs and alcohol. But soon it became a reality that was impossible to run from or cast aside.

I was draft bait. I was of age, not at university, and they were calling every able-bodied young man up. Every time I'd watch TV, I would hear the numbers of the men being drafted. I knew it'd be my turn soon enough, whether I liked it or not.

On each city block at the time sat a recruiting station, a small hut assembled on the street corner. The army men inside encouraged you to enlist. One day in 1968, after I'd just turned 18, I could no longer take the waiting. I could no longer stand my future being decided for me—so I took it into my own hands.

My heart raced, but I didn't hesitate. If I was going to be dragged into something, I'd rather walk in first.

I was not afraid. I strode with purpose two blocks down from my apartment and went straight up to the recruiter sitting in that booth. Without any greeting, I said, "I would love to serve my country, but I'm really against the war. I *don't* want to be killing anybody. I can't kill anyone. What can you do for me?"

This question taught me one of the greatest lessons: *you never know if you don't ask.* Just like I'd asked the shoeshiner all those years ago where I could get a footstool like his, my question to the recruiter changed my life just the same. I would have never known that what happened next was possible if I hadn't boldly asked the question first.

"What can you do for me?" That question became a lifelong habit. Ask first. Let the world answer. Then decide if it's worth stepping in.

The recruiter told me I could become a conscientious objector. I didn't know what the hell that was at the time; I just knew that I didn't want to carry a gun and kill people. But he educated me on the term, explaining that it was someone who refused to participate in military action due to strong moral or ethical beliefs against war or violence. Yeah, that sure sounded like me.

It felt like someone had finally put a name to the knot in my stomach—like all the confusion and dread had a direction now.

So what were my options then as a conscientious objector?

The recruiter was hung up on the fact that I didn't have any formal schooling. By that point, I'd gotten my GED. But I hadn't gone off to college.

"Listen, I have my GED, and I'm smart."

"Sorry, kid, that's not gonna cut it."

This recruiter was concerned. I wasn't. I knew I was willing to put in the work. The recruiter stood there in his army fatigues, realizing I wasn't going to take no for an answer. He looked me up and down, and with a resigned sigh said, "There is one option."

"Good, I'll take it," I replied impatiently, before he even got the words out.

"You can go down to Fort Hamilton," the recruiter continued. "They're going to give you a series of tests to find out what you're capable of as far as military training goes."

What he didn't say at the time was that there were 110 schools within the military to teach folks to become specialized. He didn't say that the potential opportunities there were endless. I just figured, what the hell, I'll go take these tests, and maybe I'll become a mechanic or something. As long as I didn't have to carry a gun, it sounded good to me.

I sure didn't know that one option was to become an astronaut.

The Compass was Internal

I spent three days at Fort Hamilton in Brooklyn and another at Fort Wadsworth in Staten Island. Each day, I sat at the small wooden school desk and took hours and hours of tests of all kinds. They asked me *everything*. I found some of the questions rude and simpleminded. Others were psychological, aimed at determining your mental fitness and emotional triggers.

I answered them all honestly.

It took a full week to get my results. Every day, I'd anxiously check the mail for my results or for a draft letter. The latter would take control over my future entirely out of my own hands.

Every day I checked, but no letters awaited me. And every day my mother said, "Bill, what are you going to do? What are you going to do? I don't want you to be involved in this crazy war!"

I didn't want to be either.

Seven days later, the recruiter called. "Well, how did I do?" I asked.

His only reply: "I need you to come down here." I didn't know what that meant, but I told him I was on my way. I was only 18. I knew nothing about how the army worked. *Were they going to grab me and say, "You failed, Bill, and we're shipping you off to Vietnam tonight?"* I had no idea, but I assumed the worst.

I walked down to the small recruitment booth. The recruiter saw me coming and, with a hint of amusement, called out, "Would you like to become an astronaut?"

I thought he was joking, a twisted, sarcastic joke. Was he mocking me? But, no, he was serious.

He brought out his comprehensive pamphlet and pointed to #93 out of the 110 military schools available—"learning how to become an astronaut," it said. Turns out, I'd done exceptionally well. My test scores said I had a 144 IQ. That qualified me to choose from any of the schools on the list.

My first thought? *How can I become an astronaut? I'm too stupid to become an astronaut.* I didn't have a formal education. I didn't think I had the book smarts to not fail straight away at school number 93. I told the recruiter as much, and he nodded his head. So we pivoted.

For the next few hours, we went over every single school and all the possibilities that were open to me. The ones we kept coming back to was becoming a food inspector and veterinary technician or vet tech. In the army, those two jobs are one and the same—many foods have animal origins, and healthy animals bear healthy food.

My years helping out Vinny and Barney at their fruit and vegetable store meant that I knew food. And my years working for Alan at the lab meant that I knew how to draw blood and had a whole slew of other skills that would help me do well as a vet tech. Plus, I loved all animals, even the mice that skittered across my apartment floor, which I'd released back into the wild as a young boy of only seven. This was the right position for me, and I said yes to joining up.

I have incredible respect for anyone who serves to protect the American people. This respect is steadfast and has never wavered. I held that respect with me at the young age of 18, and I still hold it today. Everyone who enjoys living here should have a great deal of respect for anyone who serves.

This was my way to put that respect forward, to serve, while still honoring my internal compass. So, I didn't read the contract the recruiter drew up; I just signed it. I trusted that this was a personal turning point, that it was not a defeat or betrayal to my story, because turning points in life force reinvention.

Little did I know, I was about to go from a boy to a man quickly; everything about my story was about to change.

I was off to boot camp and then off to Chicago to study to become a food inspector for the army. And that meant that I wouldn't have to carry a gun, and I wouldn't have to shoot a fellow human, innocent or not. I could uphold my values while helping my country.

So no, I didn't read the fine print before signing.

It was a mistake that would almost cost me my status as a conscientious objector and force me to fight for my values.

A Quiet Reflection: Most kids have parental guidance. Me? I had the street as guidance. I was steering the ship out in open sea, without a compass, without a map, before anyone should have let me behind the wheel.

Before I officially became a man, I already knew the thrill of success. I was familiar with captaining my own ship. But I was also living a dangerous life, white capped waves threatening to pull my boat under. I towed the line between danger and success, always staying just on the right side of it all.

For this reason, I never felt like a kid, not really. I was always one of the adults, an old soul, holding conversations with men twice my age. I had a wise mind to keep the boy in me from following the current downstream.

Not too far, I'd remind myself. Change course, go somewhere new, somewhere better. I always had that compass, that internal navigation system born from instinct. For me, what I was building meant too much to step over the line, to abandon my future for the thrill of momentary danger. But I watched as many of my friends strode boldly over that line and could not pull themselves back from it.

I watched as they forgot that life meant too much.

For The Reader: *There is nothing wrong with walking without a map. And if you stumble? Good. That means you're moving. If you change course? Even better. It means you're thinking.*

*The key is to **never trade your compass for someone else's map.***

Sometimes it's better, in fact, to choose a path and follow it, wherever it may lead. Then, of course, correct it if you must.

As you're walking and following that path, take chances, take risks, yes. But be smart about them. Become "the thinker."

Think, decide, act. Think, decide, act.

What happens based on those decisions becomes your story.

Always hold tight to your compass, and your story will unfold before you. Exactly as it was always meant to. Far more bold, daring, and varied than you could ever imagine.

Chapter Three

Still Me, Even in Uniform

---

*"Nobody handed me a blueprint. I learned by doing,
failing, and starting again."*
−Bill

The Draft Letter

I thought the army screwed me over.

The day after I signed my contract, the same contract that said I could be a conscientious objector, I opened my mailbox to find a draft letter waiting for me. It read that I was to report for duty immediately. No mention of my status as a conscientious objector.

My heart leaped into my throat. *What did this mean? Was my contract null and void? Would I have to carry a gun?* The letter was dated, postmarked, and on its way to me before I signed my contract. I'd been drafted. *Was I too late? One day too late?*

Winded, terror building, I ran to ask the recruiter, "I got my draft letter. They called me up. What do I do?!"

The recruiter didn't even blink. He looked me square in the eye and clapped me on the back, "You're all set, kid. You're good, nothing to worry about. You have your contract. It's turned in already. We honor that."

To this day, I can still feel the sigh of pure relief at his words, like a sense memory etched beneath my skin. I might go to Vietnam, yes. But I would go on my own terms.

Two weeks. I had two weeks to the day from signing my contract before I was to report for basic training.

My girlfriend at the time, Susan, had a wonderful personality and topaz blue eyes, more startling than the clearest sky. The first thing you looked at was her eyes. The next was probably her chest. She was well-liked by everyone for her high-spirited, jovial personality.

Susan wanted to send me off with the biggest farewell. She helped my mother and my friends plan party after party for me. Every day for two weeks, there was a party. Everyone I knew and loved came together to wish me well before I set off to serve my country.

I ate so much good food. I was in good shape, but I think I gained about 60 pounds from my mother's baked beans, my cousin's fried chicken, and Susan's insistence that I have "just one more!"

When those two weeks had passed, reality came for me. But I was not afraid. I had chosen this. I had chosen a path, and I was committed to seeing where it might lead.

The Man I Met in the Mirror

I reported to Fort Hamilton, a military base situated not far from my home on the southwest corner of Brooklyn. I reported in my casual clothes to a man dressed in crisp, pressed army fatigues, and he checked my name off on a clipboard.

It was as simple and anticlimactic as that.

Along with a bunch of other young guys my age, I filed onto a military bus. For 12 hours, they hauled us the long miles from Brooklyn down to Fort Jackson in South Carolina for eight weeks of basic training. The only sounds we heard were the bumps of the road and the whistling through the cracks in the windows.

I didn't do much talking. None of us did. There was a low level of anxiety that kept us all quiet. *What's coming next? What's involved? How are our lives going to change?* They were all very real questions that I didn't have answers to. I just had to follow the path and wait and see how it unfolded before me.

When that big metal bus screeched to a final halt, the driver dropped us off at an annex. The group of us stood in that big, open one-story building where officers handed out our supplies and stood at the ready with hair clippers.

They stripped me down to nothing. Then they dressed me like my sisters used to dress their dolls. But we were not playing dress up here. I knew that this was very real. My days would never look quite the same as they did back in Brooklyn.

First, every man who walked off that bus was given the same haircut. When it was my turn to step up to the guy holding the buzzer, he shaved it all off in 30 seconds. The fastest haircut of my life.

That first day stripped me of more than my hair. It stripped my assumptions. It stripped my ego. And maybe that was the point. To build a soldier—you deconstruct a civilian first.

They gave us everything we were to wear, down to our underwear. I got a pair of heavy leather boots, three changes of pressed army green clothing, a hat, and socks. They gave me a big green duffel bag made of thick, sturdy fabric to carry everything in. All I was reduced to was the duffle and the brand-new fatigues I now wore. The exact same as everyone else. The independent identity I'd had since I was a young boy—an identity of fending for myself, doing it all by myself— would not serve me here. I wasn't Bill from Brooklyn anymore. I was just another GI.

Here I was part of something different. *Something bigger.*

I Didn't Run; I Became

Next, they piled us all into an army green two-ton truck. The thing had these big, impenetrable tires and a stark white star on each of its two metal doors. We all threw our duffels into the truck and then hauled ourselves up the five feet from the ground into the back of the truck. The guy before me gave me a hand, and in turn, I gave a hand to the next guy—the camaraderie amongst us built from the very first moments.

The truck was covered by a single swath of large green canvas. When we were all inside, they closed that canvas around the back, blocking out all the light. We sat there in the pitch dark as the large truck rumbled to life and then started to move. We drove and drove. To where I didn't know. No street signs. No skyline. The city was gone. I couldn't see anything, couldn't get my bearings. I did not know this place. I had no control.

As it turns out, that was exactly the point.

We drove around for about two hours when, in reality, the base was only a 15-minute drive away. But psychologically, after those two hours, we all felt like they'd brought us to the middle of nowhere, like we had no place to go, other than where they told us to. They weren't driving us far; they were driving us deep into insecurity. We had to need each other; there was no one else.

More importantly, we felt like we had nowhere to run. After all, where would we run to? Going AWOL—absent without leave—wasn't an option in this middle of nowhere place. And that was exactly as it was designed.

The truck braked suddenly, coming to a neck-snapping halt. The master sergeants ripped the back canvas open and just started yelling, barking orders, screaming to intimidate, to demand obedience.

Each young man before me attempted to safely climb down off the truck—sitting on their butts and then scooting down the bed of the truck until their flailing feet touched the solid ground below. The master sergeants screamed and screamed that they were too slow.

I decided to take a different approach. I would not be too slow. I always aimed to get 100 on any test, and this, I knew, was a test. So, I tossed my duffle bag over my shoulder and leaped off the truck, like I was jumping off a diving board into forgiving waters below.

Not good enough.

The master sergeant kicked me in the butt to move ahead and screamed that I still wasn't fast enough. I looked around, blinking against the light, and attempted to get my bearings. Trees stretched as far as the eye could see in every direction. Everywhere I looked, it was just trees and rivers. Trees and rivers. A far cry from the city streets of Brooklyn.

Marching Toward Myself

That was day one of basic.

Day two and every day after that started with a guy banging a wooden spoon with all his might on a metal pot. It was the most unwelcome alarm clock, but it was effective.

Day after day, I'd jump out of my bunk as soon as I heard that pot clanging and stand at attention at the end of my bed. Even if you were still as a statue, quiet as the smallest field mouse, they'd still walk up to each of us, one by one, nose to nose, practically spitting in our faces:

"Who do you think you are, boy?!"

It didn't make a difference what answer you gave. We were all boys here. And every order was a strategic tactic to turn us from boys to men. To this day, I credit my time at basic training to doing just that. As harrowing and challenging as this time was, I learned a lot about myself.

We'd run outside, stand at attention, and do push-ups when they screamed at us to do so.

"GET DOWN ON THE GROUND, NOW, AND GIVE ME 50!"

We counted out loud as we did—*One drill sergeant, two drill sergeant, three drill sergeant….*

"Seymour, give me 10 more!"

I did.

"Why do you go so slow, boy? Give me 20 more!"

I did.

"Give me 30 more!"

I never blinked.

It didn't matter if we did 30 or 300 push-ups; if we gave up at any point, we failed. They pushed us to exhaustion over and over, until we realized that what our minds said was our limit, our stopping point, was not. They pushed us until we could circumvent that instinct to give up and push through just one more…just one more. The numbers never stopped; only our will remained.

They proved to us, to me, that you can *always* do one more. Never give up. Ever!

Just one more.

Eight weeks of slop and beans eaten off metal trays in the chow hall. Eight weeks of chores and early mornings. Eight weeks of physical tests that pushed us beyond our mental limits.

We trained with M16s. With .45 calibers. With grenades.

I had never shot a gun in my life and would never use one on a human. But they required me to learn how to shoot in basic training. Little did I know that this skill I did not want to have would one day save my life in Vietnam.

Everybody's shooting pattern was all over the place. Some people missed. Some had years of experience. But my pattern was right in the center. I'd never shot a gun in my life, and as a conscientious objector, I never imagined I would have to.

But I shot expert level on day one, hitting my targets right through the bullseye. Just like I could feel the pulse in the vein at Alan's laboratory to do a perfect blood draw every time, I could feel when to pull that trigger on that M16 to hit dead center, my hand-eye coordination never failing me.

When I told my commanders, my comrades, that I'd never shot a gun before, they didn't believe me. "There's no way. You have to have shot before. There's just no way," they whispered.

We trained by stepping into chambers filled with tear gas and then being locked inside until we could push past the deep burn in our lungs, master our minds, not to run, but to stay and bear it. Or until we vomited. Most people vomited. Panic was instinct. Endurance had to be learned.

I passed that test. And then they made me prove I could do it again. And then again.

The military takes a kid and makes him a man by giving him impossible task after impossible task to build up confidence in himself. My confidence in my capabilities, the mastery of my mind, was building.

The Colonel's Final Line

After eight weeks, I completed basic training. They sent me to Chicago to one of the best military schools in the world to study food inspection as my contract dictated. I was to go from a grunt—someone who's only completed basic—to somebody with a *title*.

There were about 40 or 50 of us grunts who were now all seated in neat lines of wooden school desks, anticipating our first day. I asked myself the same questions I did before basic training. *What's coming next? What's involved? How are our lives going to change?*

I was ready for whatever the answer may be—so I thought!

The colonel strolled in. He was stern, tall, and all business. The first question he asked us, his voice booming through the silent room, "How many people here have PhDs?"

A bunch of hands went up.

How many have master's? A few more hands.

"How many people have four-year degrees?" A bunch more hands went up.

"How many people don't have a college degree?" Two hands went up. My own and some fella at the back of the room.

He, at least, had a high school diploma. I only had my GED. The colonel looked us both up and down, and with a sigh said, "You two, I want to see you in my office after class." He continued on as if nothing was amiss. For the duration of class, he walked us through the structure of the course, what was expected of us, and how hard we needed to work to succeed here. Then handed us a very large manual and said, "Study it well."

After class, I walked down to the colonel's office as instructed. He sat behind a sprawling dark wooden desk, that was neatly organized, not so much as a stray pen fallen out of line. He wasted no time as the other student and I both sat down in the two empty chairs.

"Listen," the colonel said with a resigned sigh. "I wish you boys luck here, I really do. But this is very hard. The people here? They're very intelligent people. Very intelligent."

The meaning of his words hung in the air; it was like a slap in the face. He didn't think we were smart enough, or educated enough, to succeed here. But I knew from all the tests that I took back in Brooklyn, the tests that got me here in the first place, that I was smart. More than that, I had street smarts far beyond those of men twice my age.

"As I told you in class," he said, "there will be an exam every single Monday. If you fail one exam, you're still here. If you fail two, you're out. Your contract is null and void."

I opened my mouth to object—this was the first time I was hearing about this. But he cut me off with a raised hand, "It's outlined in your contract."

I didn't know it was in my contract because I didn't read it. I'd been so eager not to have to carry a gun, I would have signed my name to almost anything. It turned out there were steep requirements to stay within the parameters of that contract. And I had to meet every single one.

"Good luck, soldier." He stood, signaling that the conversation was over. His dismissive attitude was insulting, yes. It was also motivating. He didn't know me; he didn't know what I was capable of.

He talked to me like I was going to fail. But I'd show him. I was going to succeed.

Determination is a Living Flame

Sometimes when you set out to prove yourself, you don't necessarily do so on your first go at it. This was the case for me in Chicago. I was young, in love, and hadn't seen Susan since before basic training. It had been over eight weeks since I'd looked into her swimming blue eyes, matched her broad smile, or shared a warm kiss. At 18, there was no question, I had to see her. I just had to.

As soon as we got to Chicago, they told us we were allowed to travel, every weekend, if we wanted to. As a member of the army, I could fly anywhere for free. It would cost me nothing to go see Susan; I just had to be back in Chicago by Monday morning. As far as I was concerned, it was an easy decision; I could study for my first exam later. I wasn't going to fail.

Off I went to O'Hare Airport to set off back east.

Susan and I had a great time that weekend. We met our friends out at clubs, danced the night away, and laughed deeply.

Returning to Brooklyn, returning home, fed me in a way I'd missed over the last few months., in a way I needed. But all too soon, it was time to board the plane back to Chicago.

I pulled out my heavy-bound textbook for the first time on that plane ride back. Not a moment before. I didn't think I needed to. How much could I really be expected to know? We hadn't even had our first real class yet.

By the time I landed and climbed into my bunk for the night, it was 4:00 a.m. The test started at 9:00 a.m.

This was one of the only times in my life that I didn't aim for 100 prior to sitting down and putting pen to paper. I hadn't prepared as much as I could have, and I felt it.

75 was passing. I got a 72.

I failed that first exam. The first strike against me. If I failed again, I could not be a conscientious objector, I would not have my job as a food inspector for the army, and I would be required to take up arms and go wherever they sent me. This was not baseball where you get three strikes—one more and I was out.

Once again, the colonel called me into his office. Once again, he dismissed my intelligence, my capabilities. Once again, he underestimated me.

I could admit my failure to prepare here. It wasn't an intelligence failure, but rather the misgivings of a kid who was keeping one foot back in Brooklyn. It was time to take accountability. It was time to grow up. This failure did not shake me. It did not stop me. It only fueled my determination. My anger at the colonel's dismissive attitude *fueled me.* Just as I decided at the age of seven that I would become something more, I decided that day in the colonel's office, too, that I would become something more. This meant too much not to. It wasn't luck. It was work. It was sacrifice. It was deciding who I would become—and not backing down.

For the next six months, I never left my bunk. I didn't go back to Brooklyn, and I didn't see Susan. I sat there every night after class, every morning before class, with my eyes focused on that textbook. My mind committed, my hands steady. The rest of my class would go out on the weekends. They stopped asking if I wanted to join them. They knew the answer.

No, I need to study.

Every spare moment I had, I studied. And every Monday morning at 9:00 a.m. sharp, I was seated at that desk, ready and prepared. Test after test, I passed. That second failure could not touch me. I didn't care if I graduated by the skin of my teeth. I would graduate.

Each test, I aimed for 100, and I'll never forget the first time I got it. The colonel handed me my graded exam, 100 written in neat red ink in the top right-hand corner, "Congratulations," he huffed. "Let's hope it's not luck."

I graduated second in my class.

That's not luck. That's persistence, relentless determination, and a confidence in myself that I had what it took to succeed.

Little did I know how much that confidence would save my life as I was about to be tossed into the jaws of war.

__A Quiet Reflection:__ I did not have a say in whether or not I was going to war. But I did have a say in how I did it. And because of that, it turned out to be one of the best, most formative things I've done in my entire life.

It changed my life dramatically.

I could have said, I am the boy who saves bugs from my sister's flyswatter, pigeons with broken wings, and stray cats without a home. I cannot go to this place of violence.

I never wanted to disturb living things, and from what I saw on TV, that is all I perceived war to be. But I did not run or desert. I did not flee from my circumstances.

I didn't wait. I chose a different story. It reshaped everything I believed about myself—and what I was capable of.

__For The Reader:__ It's not luck. It's the sum of every refusal to quit.

If you're facing something that you feel is beyond your control, do not run from it. Instead, ask what it has to teach you. You don't need perfect conditions. You need to make a decision. You need momentum. You need one reason to say: not today— I'll keep going.

__Because life happens when it does.__

You do not get a say on the timing of when the fork in the road appears. But you do get full agency over the direction you choose to head.

Whether the story ahead looks bleak or uncertain, remember— you're still the author. Choose boldly. If needed, choose again. Just never stop writing.

You have an open invitation to choose a different story. Do not be afraid to choose. If it turns out wrong, choose again.

Chapter Four

Where the Tour Began and the Boy Ended

"What mattered wasn't skill. It was motion. Forward. Always."
—Bill

Straight Toward the Flames

The sky was on fire. Bombs split the earth beneath us, turning soil into shrapnel and smoke. The airfield we were supposed to land on was no longer a landing strip. It was a battlefield. For nearly two hours, our plane circled above the madness, searching for a safe break that never came. Then the pilot's voice cut through the roar: "We're running out of fuel. We have to land." He nosed the aircraft toward the flames, and down we went. I clenched the armrests and held my breath, bracing for impact as the war swallowed us whole.

I'd come to Vietnam as a food inspector, a conscientious objector who thought he'd found the safest path through a war.

That night, descending through the smoke and the gunfire, I understood something no recruiter's pamphlet had ever told me: sometimes the path you choose still leads you straight into the fire.

After graduating in Chicago, I was promoted to Private Second Class (PSC) and assigned a high-stakes, fast-paced role in Bayonne, New Jersey, at the Military Ocean Terminal as a food inspector. With each signature, I greenlit billions in food purchases to sustain US forces worldwide—Army, Navy, Air Force, Marines, and Coast Guard. It was my signature that fed them all.

I thought I was set. I had a prominent position doing great work three and a half days a week, with my regular pay and a housing and subsistence allowance. I could see Susan every night and every weekend, and I wasn't far from my family and friends. As far as enlistment went, I couldn't complain. Then one day, completely out of the blue, the order came.

I was going to Vietnam.

The only thing I knew about war was what I'd seen on TV. Flying into Cam Ranh Bay, I was immediately faced with the reality of war and the impact of moments that stay with you forever.

It was not at all like what I'd seen on TV.

The response to the second Tet Offensive, a series of surprise attacks by the Viet Cong forces, was raging. Below us, bombs and explosions were going off all over the place. Our plane circled above the fighting forces, the orange glow of fire burning through trees, buildings, and people and lighting up the night black countryside below.

It was too dangerous to land. For two hours, it was too dangerous to land.

Until suddenly, the pilot announced, "We're running out of fuel." I knew that it was not a good time to descend into the chaos, but running out of fuel? What choice did we have? Our plane flew straight towards the flames as the pilot attempted to land. He pulled up, banked left, unsuccessful. There was just so much commotion below. We would need to try again.

He pulled a U-turn, looking for our window to get on the ground safely. This time, I could see the runway below us as we descended. Some things you brace for. Some things brace you. When the plane's tires touched the ground and we finally came to a stop, I breathed a heavy sigh of relief. But the danger was not over. Not yet.

We needed to get to safety.

Along with the other military men on my plane, we deplaned and ran across the tarmac, heads ducked and mouths quiet as our legs moved us fast towards two awaiting buses.

The military base I was stationed at was currently in the midst of combat. We were not going to wait until it was over. Instead, we had to drive straight towards it. Bombs boomed earth-shatteringly loud outside the bus, and nearby explosions made it a harrowing drive to base. But we made it.

This was day one and my very first impression of war. As a conscientious objector, I didn't want to fight, I didn't want to kill people, and I didn't want to bear witness to destruction. But I was forced to look, forced to watch it all unfold.

That night, I met the sky in flames and the soil trembling beneath it. These were my new teachers now. And I was here to learn.

The day I landed was one of the worst days in the Vietnam War.

Most other days were so unlike that first one. Most days, it was sort of like you were in a country where you were aware war was going on, and you lived inside a perimeter, a bubble. But you were still in a combat zone.

The war was a tangible thing, but a distant one for the most part.

The Fight

There are many memories I hold about my time in Vietnam. Some I regard fondly, life lived and lessons learned that I couldn't possibly have gotten elsewhere. Some stirred me from sleep for years afterwards, jarring me awake in a damp sweat and begging me to remember where I was, who I was, and that I was not there anymore. But one memory always comes to the forefront of my mind as a moment in time that completely reshaped my journey.

The fight that changed everything.

A few months in, we were playing cards as we did most nights, up on the second floor of the barracks. A rotation of my fellow soldiers dealt hands, making bets, and playing poker. On this particular night, I was seated around the table with a few guys. One was Keith, a big, burly guy and well-known bully, a criminal who'd been given a choice between joining the army and spending two years in Vietnam or spending the next 15 years in prison.

He chose Vietnam. His choice, not mine.

There were many there, just like Keith, and the best you could do was avoid them so they wouldn't frag you in the middle of the night. Fragging was when they threw a grenade into your bunk if they didn't like you.

So, one night, Keith smiled at me across the table, his two silver teeth gleaming in the lamplight. He thought he had a good hand. I knew I had better: ace, king, queen, jack, and ten. I had a royal flush, or as I liked to call it, a super hand. I had him beat. I threw my hand down, then I reached in and took the whole pot without breaking eye contact. I watched as his smile was immediately replaced with unfettered anger. Keith jumped up, screaming, "You're a cheater, Seymour. You're a cheater! Cheater!"

"Fuck you," I responded without a trace of fear, standing to match him, as I looked him dead in the eye. Keith was a bully to almost everyone else, but he'd never messed with me before. I didn't think winning a game of cards fair and square would change that. I was wrong.

In three steps, Keith had crossed to my side of the table and punched me square in the nose. Hard. It hurt like hell. I bled all over the place. I thought he broke my nose. I was dizzy and felt like I was going to black out. Keith wasted no time; now out in the open hallway that overlooked two stories of barracks, he continued to scream, "Seymour's a cheater! He's a cheater!" for all the men below to hear.

My temper was really raging now. How dare this *bully* talk about me that way? I'd played a fair game! I always played a fair game, and he knew it. Blood streaming out of my nose and down my face; I didn't hesitate. I walked out to that hallway, pulled back my fist, and snapped it with force towards Keith's face. The blow hit him square in the nose and was so unexpected that he stumbled back a few steps.

I saw it coming. There was nothing I could do to stop it. Keith's back hit the railing, and he fell backwards off the second-floor balcony and down two stories to the barracks below. He hit the ground with a muffled thunk. Only a breath passed before he screamed, "My back! My back! Owww, my back."

All of the men around me ran down the stairs to where Keith now laid. I barreled after them to make sure he was okay. I hadn't wanted to hurt him; I'd just wanted to give him a taste of his own medicine.

When my feet hit the ground floor landing, I crouched down to where Keith was sprawled out. "Are you okay? Are you okay?" He looked me in the eyes, his own nose now bleeding, sat up, and in one swift motion, punched me again. This time, his fist landed right at the bridge of my already-bleeding, swollen nose right between my eyes. It took me a few moments to shake away the blurry vision, the sheer shock, before rage overtook me.

I was against violence, against hurting another. But his fist sparked my temper and turned me into a living flame. I just started swinging.

I don't know how or when I'd moved, but I sat with a knee on either side of Keith's torso. I kept beating the shit out of him, knocking the two silver teeth from his mouth, until one of my first sergeants walked up, commanding order. He was a big guy. He pulled me by my shirt right off Keith, as my arms kept swinging, now failing to hit their target.

When my temper started to reduce from a boil to a simmer, and my mind began to clear, I knew, I just knew I was in trouble. *They're going to throw me in the brig,* I thought.

I knew I'd screwed up. My first sergeant knew I'd screwed up.

But he also knew that Keith was a bad guy, and that this hadn't happened unprovoked. My captain knew it as well. I was a good guy. I proved myself every day and was a team player. So instead of sending me to jail, they sent me far, far away out to the middle of nowhere to Tuy Hoa Air Base. It was their way of keeping me out of the brig, and I was grateful for it.

At the time I wasn't sure if this was exile or my evolution. But little did I, or they, know, it was a decision that would change the course of my life forever.

The Doctors

Because I was the only one from my unit stationed so far out, I was given my own hooch—a little hut and my new living quarters—which was fashioned from a big, round piece of metal. There was a door on one end, a door on the other, and no windows. That was it. It wasn't glamorous, but it was mine.

They sent me here to escape the repercussions from what I did to Keith, yes. But also, because it was close to a veterinary clinic that housed 47 military dogs. Not only was I trained as a food inspector, *but also* as a veterinary technician. I could be useful there.

Near me lived a group of military doctors who had a beautiful place, far nicer than my hooch. It was right across from the hospital, the perfect location that allowed them to drop everything and run over any time a medivac came in. It was a small resort built by the Seabees—a nickname for the United States Naval Construction Battalions—back in '63.

Every day, I could smell the doctors cooking hamburgers, the scent wafting over to my hooch on the breeze. They smelled incredible and made my mouth water, so I said as much. When I saw one of the doctors coming out of the house, I stopped him. "Boy, that food smells so good," I said.

He looked me up and down and noticed the medical insignia on the lapel of my shirt, with an approving smile, said, "Come on over and have a hamburger. Introduce yourself to all the doctors." So, I did, and that was it. They opened the door, and I didn't hesitate to walk in.

The doctors liked my company, and I was nurtured and fueled by theirs. When they found out I was a food inspector, they asked me, "Hey Bill, do you think you could get some steaks for us?" Hamburgers were good and reminded us all of home. But steaks? Now, that was *living*.

"Absolutely," I told them without question. It was pretty simple. I'd just say a couple cases of steaks were getting old, put my name on it, and I could walk out with them. So that's exactly what I did. We called it "force issuing."

After spending lots of time with them in the compound and over in the hospital, I became true friends with the doctors. I lived nearby, I could force issue some food, and I was good company. They, in turn, gave me the best education of my life and a wealth of knowledge through nonstop conversation.

We played bridge every night, and the conversation flowed as we played. Surrounded by brilliant minds, I soaked in every word, learning from their expertise, their insight, their education, and their hard-earned wisdom. I observed how their egos often kept them from learning from each other. But unlike them, I had no barriers, no preconceived notions that I knew it all.

Our nights were filled with clanking glasses of bourbon and cognac, puffs of smoke from Cuban cigars, and indulging in fancy snacks sent by their wealthy parents. It was a world unlike any I had known. My mind changed around what was possible for me after this war.

They taught me about life, about living, and about possibility, and that I wasn't just a conscientious objector or even a food inspector. I could be anything. And I was already becoming someone new.

Whenever a medivac helicopter touched down on the landing pad across the street, we left our merriment and sprang into action. It didn't matter that I was a food inspector; when I was with the doctors, I was one of them. And through their knowledge, their teaching, I knew a lot. I knew how to *do* a lot.

We'd run across the street right as the medivac was about to touch down. You could hear its speed and knew it was time. "Bill, grab his arm!" I did. "Seymour, secure his leg!" I did that too, even if that arm or leg was not still attached to the body.

It was an intense, unforgettable chapter in my life. One that shaped me in ways that I'll carry forever. I learned that education doesn't just come from street smarts or school desks. I learned so much from my time in Tuy Hoa.

Observe, think, listen, think.

Until the Barrel Turned White

While I often stayed over at the doctors' compound, I also had a bed at the veterinary clinic I worked in, half a mile from the outskirts of the main base. I was responsible for caring for the animals on the base and overseeing all 47 of the sentry dogs stationed at Tuy Hoa Air Base. I often stayed alone at the clinic when I worked too late to travel back to my hooch or when I was needed overnight to monitor the dogs.

One such night, I was sound asleep on my little cot at the clinic. Within the darkness, all 47 of the dogs *erupted*—barking, snarling, and growling at something beyond the perimeter. It was common for a few of the dogs to bark at wild animals that passed by in the night or at small explosions in the distance. But this was different.

This was a warning. There was something wrong, and they felt it.

Sleep left me instantly; my mind was clear, and my eyes were searching. Something was very wrong. The clinic was pitch black inside, not a single light was left on, and no one was inside but me. Outside, the field beyond was blanketed by the black night, and darkness stretched beyond the perimeter like an abyss.

I pulled back the thick curtain that was on the window—which always stopped the hot sun from making it uncomfortable inside during the daylight hours—and peered past the barbed wire. Then, I saw them: Viet Cong advancing. Dozens, perhaps hundreds, of men cloaked by darkness, whose forms were just barely visible. I might have missed them if the dogs hadn't sounded their alarm. It definitely would have been over for me.

Fear isn't something I feel often. But at that moment, it hit me hard. I was completely on my own. Not a soul was with me. It was me against the enemy. I thought I was about to die, be overrun, or worse, be captured. *I couldn't be captured. I just couldn't.* I watched, completely still, my breath frozen in my lungs, as they began cutting through the perimeter barbed wire that divided our sides.

No. No. I would not go out like this. I refused to be a sitting duck. I might be a conscientious objector, but I didn't have to kill a single soul to hold my own.

Although fear threatened to overtake me, I did not let it paralyze me. I didn't wait for help. I didn't run. I took action.

My thoughts took hold: *It's about survival. I just want to live. I love life.*

I slid down from the window and grabbed my M16, the automatic rifle that lived under my small cot, and pulled it out from underneath. My other hand reached for the three boxes of ammunition that I knew were also under that bed until I felt them and pulled them free. There was no time to think. My basic training came back to me in a wave so powerful that my hands moved independent from my fear-stricken mind.

I returned to my perch at the window, with my gun loaded, and the remaining boxes of ammo neatly lined up on the windowsill for easy access. I switched the M16 to automatic, then stuck the barrel of the gun out the window and just started shooting, not to hit a target, but to make noise—a whole lot of noise.

I hoped the sound would carry half a mile to my comrades and bring support.

I could barely see the Viet Cong in the murky darkness. So, I just kept sweeping the gun back and forth, blindly firing into the night air.

My finger remained pressed down on the trigger. My relentless gunfire echoed through the night like an entire battalion was behind me. Clip after clip—loaded, fired, emptied, replaced.

It was just me, one man who refused to back down. But to the Viet Cong, it must have sounded like there were 50 guys waiting and prepared to fight them.

Boom. Reload. Boom. Reload. Boom.

The barrel turned white from the heat as round after round fired from that gun. The heat radiated through the rifle into my hand. Even as my hand began to warm and my fingers began to blister, I did not let up on that trigger.

It was probably mere minutes, but it felt like hours until help arrived. Suddenly, my rounds were not the only foreboding thing sounding through the night. Flares shot up into the darkness—white ones to light the sky. Red ones were a call for support and got rid of the shadows. Three helicopters crested the trees. Guys from my side started streaming into the veterinary office, "What's going on? We heard you. We came. What's happening, Seymour?" I told them, and they too saw the Viet Cong moving just beyond the split barbed wire fence. Then they began firing.

I was no longer alone. I had done it. I had held out until help arrived.

As suddenly as the threat appeared, it was gone. The Viet Cong were overwhelmed by the many rifles now shooting at them from my side. They were swiftly pushed back; the survivors fled into the night, disappearing under the same cover of darkness from which they'd arrived.

I thought deeply, *was this karma*? Did the dogs just save my life because I was good to the mice that skittered across our apartment floor as a boy? Today, is there more behind why I love dogs so much? Is this why I connect with them so deeply?

After the war, it was this memory that followed me.

Dreams turned to nightmares, creeping into my subconscious to disturb restful sleep. I'd wake up drenched in sweat, catching myself, grounding myself in the present. But I was not always fighting the enemy in Vietnam. I was not always at war. Sometimes, I was still that young boy of seven saying "enough" to the circumstances I was born into. Sometimes the dreams were of my father, a thick leather belt in his hands. The sound was like the cracking of a whip, waking me from sleep.

But even in my worst nightmares, I remained the hero of my own story. The Viet Cong marched toward me, but I did not cower. I took control. The belt whipped towards me, and my hand shot out to grab it from my father. I took control.

Enough. I thought. *That is enough.*

The trajectory of my life is my own and is for no one's taking but mine. Waking or asleep, my mind controls the narrative.

A Quiet Reflection: After the war, I used my veteran benefits to attend college and study human behavior. That journey never truly ended. For the balance of my life, I've observed humanity in motion—quietly, daily, deliberately. I study people not to judge, but to understand. Over time, I've come to see myself as an intuitive vessel—empathic, attuned, and shaped by what others carry.

I became a witness to the human condition—quietly absorbing, quietly evolving.

But what I learned about myself, and about others, from hard-lived experience? That taught me so much more than a formal education ever did.

The doctors gave me an education that most people would beg to have. But perhaps this is only true because they always communicated to me as if I were an equal. In those moments, I was just as important as they were, just as capable. And in those moments, I chose to help.

Doctor, food inspector, veterinary technician, respectful military soldier, and a man. I chose to be Bill. Fully, wholly, and with a grateful heart.

You see, when we can learn to see ourselves on equal footing with those the world may see as superior, we allow our whole selves to be brought forth. We grow and we expand, beyond the confines of what we think is possible for ourselves.

For The Reader: *There is a conversation between what you live and what you quietly carry. When you hold a victim's story too tightly, you cannot see yourself for who you truly are. You cannot see who you have the capacity to become.*

You cannot see yourself as the hero of your own story.

The reality is: you are always one choice away from becoming the hero. But to do so, you must release yourself from your mind's own constraints.

You are no better than anyone else. You are no worse than anyone else. You are just as valuable, just as capable, just as needed.

And you certainly are not the victim. Always remember to be the hero. Because the world isn't done testing you yet.

Oh, and always be gentle with animals, caring to each other, and kind to trees, bees and tiny bugs, too. You never know when karma is watching or how it'll repay you later.

Act Two

The World and What it Taught Me

Chapter Five

The Compass Didn't Fail—It was Recalibrating

"The trick about starting over: never start with failure."
−Bill

The Ending That Felt Like a Beginning

What waited for me beyond Vietnam wasn't just another test. It was an entirely new battleground. Only this time, the fight wasn't for survival. It was for the life I hadn't even begun to imagine.

Even when I'm tested by life, failure does not follow me. It has never been something that defines me or something that festers and turns to regret. No. Failure doesn't stick. It doesn't stain. It doesn't stay.

When something doesn't work out in my favor, I pick myself up, dust myself off, and commit once again to becoming something more.

Looking back on my life with the age-old wisdom of 75 years, I don't regret a single moment, a single choice, a single thing—except for one:

> *That I didn't fully understand my capacity to love until later in life. Or that I had a deep yearning for a big family and a lively, loving home.*

It may seem simple; it may seem a stark pivot from talk of war and of dedication to becoming a man of success. But it's not a detour—it's the destination. Just as I've won and lost in my journey from boyhood to manhood, and just as I have won and lost in business (as you will see unfold in Act Three), I have also won and lost in love.

Success in love and relationships is just as valuable as success in other areas of our lives, yet it is often overlooked. We sidestep it. We downplay it. We pretend it's secondary. Instead, I believe we should look right at it with eyes opened wide and with bold hearts.

My trials and tribulations when it comes to love lost and gained were steps along the road I had to take to find something good, lasting, and pure. They are what helped shape other endeavors in my life. They made me a better man. So, while yes, it is true that I never felt like I failed in anything in life, except for love, this only made the staying power of something real and worthwhile all the sweeter.

At the time of writing, I have been happily married for 39 years. My wedding day is one of my fondest and happiest memories. And the day my daughter came into this world, her eyes locked onto mine, and it was one of the happiest moments of my life. I'll never forget when the doctor gave her to me and I sang to her, "Baby cakes, you are the sweetest little baby cakes." Or the moment years later when she sang it back to me, grinning widely.

These moments matter. They're not just sentimental—they're seismic. These moments are achievements that rival my greatest win in any other area of my life.

But I did not get to these moments without a few bumps in the road, without times that I blamed others for relationships that failed. Without hard-won lessons to be learned, and then learned again, until I finally recognized that there wasn't anybody to blame for my failures but me. Taking responsibility and holding myself accountable was the lesson I had to learn.

Like everything else in my life, success was found in the *choosing*—in the choice and understanding of what lasting love truly is and what it meant to me to have it, to claim it, and to let it in.

Yes, I have been happily married for 39 years. Yes, it has been one of the greatest successes of my life. It wasn't my first marriage that succeeded or even my second. But when Milissa walked into the racquetball club that day, everything shifted. I knew at that moment that I would do whatever it took to become a man worthy of love that lasts.

She Wasn't a Detour; She was the Destination

I first met Milissa in 1984. I remember it vividly—a moment so electric it etched itself into memory. In the early '80s, I was living the bachelor life, jet-setting back and forth to Peru to run my importing and exporting business, Charter Merchants International, and traveling the world as a competitive racquetball player. It was almost a decade after the Vietnam War ended and even more time than that since I'd returned home to Brooklyn.

I'd lived a few different lives since then, and my time with Susan was a distant memory, the end of our relationship sudden, harsh, and life-changing.

Susan and I had gotten married 15 years earlier back in 1969. The marriage lasted all of three years, most of which I was stationed in Vietnam. We had a big church wedding after I graduated from the Food Inspector Program back in Chicago, during my time in New Jersey at the Military Ocean Terminal. Susan walked down the aisle in something white, poofy, and frilly. Her six bridesmaids flanked one side of the aisle, my six groomsmen flanked the other, and 170 guests sat in the pews.

Her father walked her, achingly slow, down the long aisle to give her away, so slow that the organ player had to begin the song a second time, continuing the music until they finally reached me. Susan's father lifted her veil, kissed her on the cheek, and turned to shake my hand. As he did, he leaned in to whisper in my ear, "One day, I'm going to get my daughter back. Just you watch. *Just you watch.*"

The man was a clinically diagnosed narcissist and harbored a tendency towards emotional incest. In plain terms, he was hopelessly in love with his daughter. I'm familiar with those diagnoses now, because as both a psychiatrist and my lawyer stated three years later during our divorce proceedings, the cause for our split was "parental alienation". In his eyes, no man besides him was worthy of his daughter's love. I wasn't in that moment as he gave her away in the church, and I wasn't years later when we finally parted.

He'd show up at our apartment unannounced, belligerent, and unbelievable. He'd spout all the ways in which I'd never measure up: "You will never be a NYC cop like my two sons. You don't have what it takes. You're just a hustling kid from Brooklyn." I was only 19, and his sons were over 30. But that didn't matter to him.

Looking back, I think I knew right then, standing there in my suit and tie and looking out at our friends and family seated in the pews, that Susan and I were doomed to fail. But, I was only 19. At the time, I thought you couldn't find better for me. I thought I had clearly mapped out what a successful life looked like. And it included this. It included Susan.

I thought I knew it all.

Since I was stationed in Bayonne, New Jersey, I didn't think I was going anywhere, and surely not to Vietnam. I had a lot of responsibility in Bayonne, and there weren't many US Army Food Inspectors like me around the world—surely they'd keep me where I was most needed. I thought that was in New Jersey, a stone's throw from Brooklyn, and at home with Susan.

But I was wrong. I knew nothing about the journey that lay ahead.

Fast forward five years, life had changed a lot since Susan. I started a few businesses—sold one, lost another. I got married again to a lovely woman named Gina. It was a marriage of convenience that naturally ran its course. When it ended, there was a small part of me that was defined by the failure. Two marriages had come and gone by the time I was 25.

What did I know about love? Not enough, I thought.

At the time, I wasn't willing to try again.

Not until I met Milissa at the BQE Racquetball Club in 1984 did something within me shift. I was forever changed in an instant. She had long, black hair tumbling in waves to her shoulders, a stunning complement to her warm, chestnut brown eyes, broad, welcoming smile, and hourglass figure. A lot of women had come in and out of that racquetball club over the years, but from that moment, no one else compared.

Milissa was like a beacon calling me home.

Lonely in the Limelight

Calling me home from what, exactly? The man I'd become—"The Bachelor."

For almost a decade after my second marriage ended, I remained single. There were girls, lots of girls, but to me they were just friends. Friends who were sometimes more. But never more in the way that made me want to abandon my solidarity and fast lifestyle. I lived in a beautiful apartment in Brooklyn with a doorman and a rooftop pool. I drove a brand-new Buick Riviera. I had money, and I was always making more.

My importing and exporting business would take me down to Peru for weeks at a time, where I stayed in lavish hotels, shook hands with commanding generals of the Peruvian army, big bankers, major farmers, and other prominent figures. I was living a good life. A great life, so I thought.

When I wasn't traveling, I would rent a house in the Hamptons during the summer with six female friends. We summered there for seven years. I had always related to women better than men and I especially related to these six whip-smart women. I wasn't into playing the macho asshole like so many men my age. With women, I felt their softness, their intelligence, and their sincerity. They were smarter and better company. Men often don't like to talk honestly. Men like to hide stuff and put on a facade. But women…women talk deeply. They share. They show up. They speak truth, share their thoughts and innermost feelings, and are honest about who they are and what they want.

That was the company I liked to keep.

We had a sprawling green yard where we played games, drank, and had cup-filling conversations. We had a huge pool, ocean views, and were a short walk from the beach. On the weekends, I would invite a girlfriend down from the city. And the next weekend, I invited someone different. The next weekend, someone different.

My friends would joke around with me all the time about it. "Bill, who are you taking this weekend? Who's the girl of the week?" Because there was always someone new. Every weekend, it was a new girl—never permanent, lasting, or substantial. It was just fun and good company. And that's how I liked it.

I had women. I had pot. I had money. I was a bachelor, unapologetic and untethered.

Everyone knew that I didn't want a long-term relationship, that I wasn't interested. You wanted to be my friend? Great. You want to have sex? Great. But don't put your hooks in me because I'm going to pull them out without blinking. That's how it was for a decade. The women were always there, but I never wanted any of them. I was focused on my career, on that sole definition of success, and at the time, nothing tasted sweeter.

I'm Going to Marry That Woman

That's the man I was when Milissa walked into the racquetball club for the first time. I just finished up a match in one of the two glass-walled courts right at the front of the club. Ten more cement courts sat behind them, and a restaurant was nestled off to the side. I walked straight to my towel, which was slung across the back of a nearby chair. I started wiping the sweat off my body, casually speaking to the guy I just finished playing with, Frankie. My friend, Ray, sauntered over to join us, and we talked about our game.

Our normal routine.

The front door swung open, and Milissa strode in with purpose and an easy confidence that caught my attention. She stopped and asked someone where Bill Louie, the jiujitsu master and head instructor at the club, was. She was meeting him for her job interview.

Milissa was dressed in the classic '80s aerobics instructor leotard, tights, and matching leg warmers—they fit her like a glove. She sure looked the part, and her smile was magnetic. If it were up to me, I would have given her the job right there.

I couldn't let it go; I just kept my eye on her as she easily laughed with Bill Louie, who'd just shaken her hand and introduced himself. I heard her say, "I'm Milissa." *Milissa.* I took the mental note right then and there. I've never been good at remembering names, but hers etched itself into my mind.

There was just something about her. She was different then, and she's different now, over 40 years later. I have a sort of sixth sense that has shown up a few times throughout my life, a quiet knowing that whispers, "This matters." I don't know how or why, but I know when it does, I listen. A thread, a path, I'm meant to follow.

I knew at that moment that Milissa would become something more to me.

Ray jostled my shoulder, in an attempt to snap me out of my reverie, "Hey, come on, man, let's go. You've got enough girls. You've got enough. Come on."

I didn't hesitate; I just said, "I'm going to marry that woman."

Frankie and Ray both busted out laughing. They knew my bachelor *modus operandi*; they knew I'd sworn off marriage, off relationships, and off anything too serious or too deep.

"Yeah, okay, sure, Bill. You told me you'd never get married. Not again," Frankie said through his laughter. "What's she, #19 on your list?"

"This one's different. This one I'm going to marry."

A Quiet Reflection: I thought I failed. I tried to be a good husband, a steady, consistent force in relationships. But in those early moments, all I could see was what did not work out. I could not see that it perhaps had to fall apart, so something else could come together.

So, I set myself on a new course, one where I was independent, and did not have to face the hard questions of why something (or someone) didn't work. I didn't have to ask myself why I had even tried to force something that clearly did not fit in the first place.

Oftentimes in life, this is what we do.

We force something to work because we think we have to; we think it's what we're supposed to do and that there's no way around it.

But I've learned that forcing life's hand to fit the mold you expect will never actually reshape anything real. Instead, your heart will simply stay stagnant and closed until something cracks it open.

And something will.

For The Reader: Please don't judge me! Try never to judge anyone.

Maybe you have your own area of life where you call yourself a failure, where you feel like no matter how hard you try to make something fit, it simply doesn't.

Yesterday is gone. Stop knocking at its door.

The past is sealed—no retakes, no rewrites, no rescue. You stand in the only frame that matters: now. But if your gaze clings to the rearview, you'll miss the road unraveling beneath your feet.

Every second spent staring backward is a theft from the future you were born to shape.

History doesn't need your permission to stay dead. But the future?

The future is waiting for your hands, your voice, and your defiance. It's all yours if you're ready to stop rehearsing regret and start directing what comes next.

Let them go—both the identity of failure and the thing that does not fit. Let go of the things no one knows about but you.

Make room for movement to find you. And be open when it comes.

Because that movement may be just the thing you've been waiting for. The thing that shakes you awake. The thing that shows you that you never failed. You were just waiting for something to make you move. You were just waiting for the perfect timing when you became the person who was ready to meet the moment.

When something moves, follow it. That's where your happy ending lives.

Or maybe, your happy beginning.

Chapter Six

Sparrows Group, Eagles Fly by Themselves

Nothing in Excess

I remember the floor: hard, cold, lonely. I remember the apartment: stripped, empty, bare. I remember the other woman in the bed we shared. Yes, I remember it all too vividly, how Susan and I unraveled.

The year was 1971. I completed my service in the army, and I returned home to Brooklyn, home to Susan, and home to a world that no longer felt like mine. I was in Vietnam for 11 months, 27 days, 16 hours, and 30 seconds. So much changed in that time. I returned to a country, to a place that was foreign to my memory.

Daily protests in the streets against the war. People spitting at veterans returning home. Nonstop political fighting and different sides being taken for or against.

The discotheques were still filled with dancing, sweaty, jovial people every night—but they weren't my people. *Bill, do you know that Rusty's in prison? Do you know that Eddie committed suicide? Do you know cousin Johnny overdosed?* That one broke me. They all broke me.

The list continued. *Give me a break*, I silently pleaded in my mind, *I'm only 20 years old*. It was unreal, and I felt my heart split in two at the continued news that so many good friends of mine were no longer with us. Those friends, family, and comrades didn't have limitations. They didn't do anything in moderation. And while they had the time of their lives—it'd cost them everything.

"Nothing in excess, everything in moderation," became my new motto. Now that I was back, I was committed more than ever to *staying here*, on this earth, on the right side of the line, and where my soul was most at home—in Brooklyn.

I did not go back to working in Alan's lab or selling drugs. I wasn't the same man I was when I left, and I wouldn't repeat the same cycle. Instead, I went into business with an old neighborhood friend, Carmine. At just 20 years old, I was eager to build something meaningful for myself, and Carmine was just as ready to join me.

Together, we opened a small fruit and vegetable store in a West Indian neighborhood in Brooklyn. As a young white guy, I stood out among the predominantly Black, Jamaican,

Dominican, Haitian, and other ethnically diverse residents, including a few older Italians who had remained as the neighborhood evolved. Despite our differences, I built strong, lasting relationships with everyone in the community, and I truly loved that neighborhood. It pulsed with life and grit and heart. It was filled with incredible people. Great human beings.

Every day at 2:00 a.m., I made my way to the fish market beneath the West Side Highway in Manhattan, meticulously selecting only the freshest seafood from the hundreds of vendors there. After receiving a chit—a pick-up order receipt—my brother would later retrieve the order with our truck while I continued on to the Bronx Terminal Market around 4:00 a.m. to purchase fruits and vegetables. It was just my daily routine.

With my extraordinary education in food inspection, keen eye for quality from my time working at Barney's fruit and vegetable store, and a refined palate, I could easily distinguish the finest produce from the rest. It took me back to when I was that little boy, eyes wide and hands eager, lining up the fruit and polishing it. I loved every moment.

I took immense pride in selecting only the best fruits and vegetables, ensuring that our neighborhood, which had limited access to fresh, nutritious food, could enjoy top-tier ingredients.

By 7:00 a.m., I'd arrive at my shop, flip the sign from "Closed" to "Open," and embrace the new day. After carefully setting up the stands with an abundance of vibrant, fresh produce, I'd fire up the grill and start cooking fish right inside our little store.

The rich, savory aroma would drift through the neighborhood, drawing people like a magnet.

People would stop by just to chat, and I'd serve them a fish sandwich along with a generous bag brimming with colorful, fresh fruits and vegetables. We'd exchange stories while the shop hummed with activity. Selling well over a thousand pounds of fish each week, our store was constantly packed. Business was never a concern—it thrived because it was real. I learned quickly that when you provide people with the best, they keep coming back, day after day. Quality speaks louder than any pitch.

The shop may have been thriving, but my relationship with Susan didn't get as much of my attention. We were strained. And the truth was, we'd never gotten back to the young, wide-eyed lovers we'd been before the war. My typewritten love letters sent from Vietnam were distant and forgotten.

Each morning, I was gone before sunrise, and I didn't return home until late. Susan's father still insisted I wasn't worthy of his daughter, no matter how much my business thrived, and perhaps Susan started to listen to him. Or maybe she'd just grown bored, rebellious, and unforgiving. Maybe she'd fallen out of love. I truly can't say what it was that caused our demise, but I can mark the exact moment we ended.

I Chose Her, but Not Myself

The image stayed burned in my mind for years after I caught her in bed with another woman.

Early and unexpectedly, I came home to our beautiful brownstone apartment from my shop one afternoon. Exhausted and worn from my morning selecting produce and fish down at the docks before dawn, I called her name from the doorway, "Susan, I'm home!" And I made my way to our bedroom to rest for a while.

The wooden door opened, creaking on its hinges, to my wife, who was not alone in the bed that lay before me. My anger flared, hurt sparked, and confusion fueled me. *What was happening? How could she do this? And with her?* I didn't understand. I didn't take the time to understand. I just reacted.

We fought that afternoon. It was a loud, angry, screaming fight that perhaps shook the floorboards and caused plaster to float down from the ceiling in the apartment below just like it did when I was a little boy in my family's cramped railroad apartment, when the voices of the couple upstairs crashed through the thin walls with a rage that threatened to cave the ceiling in on top of us.

I don't know for sure. Maybe no one was home in the apartment below to hear our own rage booming above. But what I do know is that in that moment, I felt like I was that little boy again. I was at the mercy of others' choices.

I called her all kinds of names, and she spat rage-fueled insults right back at me. We both lost our temper, but at a certain point, our screaming settled down. My chest heaved with frustration and uncertainty. *Where were we supposed to go from here?* At the time, I didn't know.

Susan made that choice for me.

I left her in that apartment, crying and begging for me to listen to her, to hear her out. "I have work," I told her, "I just came home to rest for a while before I took the night shift." And honestly, I didn't want to be there anyway. I didn't want to sit in that now-tainted apartment with a woman who betrayed me. *Us.*

No, I would focus on work instead. Work was clean. Work was controllable. Work didn't lie or cheat.

So, I left.

He Took More Than Space

When I arrived back home the next morning, my hurt had settled, and my ears were open to listen. But Susan wasn't there. *Nothing* was there.

That was how we ended—*without words, without warning.*

I left for work. Susan left for her parents' house. And when I came home the next morning, the apartment was completely empty, *a ghost of itself.* Eerie. Haunted.

I felt so uneasy just being there. I felt like I couldn't breathe.

The first chance he had, the first time Susan and I were on the rocks, her father saw his chance, and he took it. I had never been the man he wanted for her. So, he enlisted his two sons to help him erase every trace of what we were. They used her key to enter the apartment while I was at work, and took *everything.*

Everything that was hers. Everything that was mine. Everything that made our house a home. *Not a trace of us remained.*

The couch, the bed, the pots and pans were all gone. Not a single fork or roll of toilet paper was left, and not a photo remained in any frame. The apartment was barren, swept clean. It didn't matter that I bought most of that stuff or that it was my apartment, my furniture, and my name on the lease. Perhaps her father saw it as retribution owed for stealing Susan away from him in the first place. No matter his logic, or lack thereof, her bitter father left me with nothing—nothing but the wood floors and stone walls to keep me company.

And a letter.

There on the kitchen counter sat a haphazardly folded piece of paper. I knew who it was from. I steeled myself before opening that letter. Inside it read:

You'll never see her again. We'll see you in court.

The Floor

Bone-tired from the night shift and drained from the turbulence of the day, I curled up on the hard wooden floor of our apartment and cried. The tears came like never before, not just because of Susan, but because I didn't recognize the man I'd become.

That night, I reflected back on my life, memories like pictures whirring through my mind: *What am I doing? What's going on? How did I get here?* When sleep finally took me, it was as if my tired mind was susceptible to my worst nightmares coming out to play.

Sleep was fitful, harsh, and harrowing. Memories I had buried clawed their way to the surface.

I'm back in Vietnam, the Viet Cong advancing, silent and swift. Like ghosts floating effortlessly through the barbed wire that is meant to keep them out.

A cacophony of sound. All 47 dogs snarling and snapping at the unseen enemy. Alone. I am entirely alone save for the M16 that's clenched between my hands, my knuckles stark white just like the barrel of the gun I fire.

I'm a conscientious objector. I'm not supposed to be here. I shouldn't be here. Sweat pools on my brow and drips into my eyes so fiercely that I can no longer see the enemy that's coming for me.

I blink against the sweaty tears. I blink again, my vision clearing. Only I'm not in Vietnam anymore. I'm back in Brooklyn, looking through the eyes not of a 19-year-old man, but of a 7-year-old child.

The chair is heavier than I expected, and almost as big as my tiny, hungry body. But I do not hesitate as I swing. My father just hit my mother. As she fell to the floor, my sisters screamed shrilly and unintelligibly, far louder than they shrieked when the mice scampered across their feet. For this is a different kind of fear. A different kind of pleading for it to stop. For it to get better.

My father turns, clenching his fists, to my sisters now cowering in the corner, "Get in the back room! Now!"

he yells at them, his voice thundering through the small, cramped kitchen. They do as they are told and run.

I do not.

I move toward him. Fearless and determined to stop the madness instead of becoming it. I clasp my tiny arms around his broad waist and try to hold my father back. He pushes me away with force, and my mother pleads with him to stop. I know he will not stop.

Although I stumble, I do not stop either.

I grab the closest thing I can find—the kitchen chair. And I swing it with everything I have, with all the force a 7-year-old boy can summon. It crashes against his back, thudding upon contact, but it does not break. I know he feels it because he freezes, slowly turning and setting his eyes upon me.

He charges.

Acting on instinct, I do the only thing I can think of: I kick him right where it hurts hard. He doubles over, face contorting in pain, and I kick him again. This time, square in the face, buying myself a few precious seconds to run across the room to where a kitchen knife sits on the stove.

I turn, mirroring my father's ferocity. I clench the knife in both hands, my knuckles stark and white against the blade. Just as my knuckles were stark and white around that M16, 12 years later.

In that moment, as a boy in Brooklyn—just like in that veterinary clinic in Vietnam—I know that no one is coming to save me. No one is coming to save us. My mother, my sisters, my brothers. No one is coming.

But I'm already here.

I am the line between chaos and safety.

I can do something, anything, to get the enemy—my father—to halt. To stop this madness and retreat. I look my father dead in the eye and command, "Get out of here."

I mean it, and he can tell.

Twice before this, I grabbed the belt from his hands when he'd been about to strike. Twice before this, I stood against the injustice he wrought—sudden, viscous, and cruel.

I would not be cruel. But I could be just as vicious. Instinct and survival written in my DNA.

In that moment, I think he sees me for the first time. Sees the boy I became under his fist. The boy who would not break.

So long as I stand between him and my mother and sisters, he cannot rule this house with the iron fist he wants. He holds my stare for three long seconds before turning and walking out the door.

My father left that day, and we didn't see him again for two whole years.

Eagles Fly by Themselves

I woke from the nightmare with a start, surging to my feet, thrown back into the present. My heaving breaths were erratic. My eyes scanned the empty Brooklyn brownstone, landing upon my crumpled jacket lying on the floor. The jacket had served as my pillow for the night. It was the only piece of clothing I had left that wasn't already on my body.

It took me a few moments to get my bearings and reorient myself in the now. Brooklyn, I was in Brooklyn. I was not in Vietnam. And I was no longer that 7-year-old boy.

Looking back, that floor was one of my lowest moments—but also one of my most defining.

My waking nightmares reminded me of who I was. And who I was not.

I lost Susan, and at the time, I wasn't willing to take any blame for it. But years later, I still thought of that floor often and what it had to teach me. Later, I got what I learned on that floor tattooed on my bicep as a constant reminder—*Sparrows group, eagles fly by themselves.*

I became the eagle.

I flew alone for years, and I was content to remain that eagle suspended in the hustle and addicted to the grind.

Perhaps, if Milissa hadn't walked into my racquetball club that fateful day in 1984—over a decade after those nightmares plagued me on the cold wooden floor—I would have kept flying solo.

But life still had a few more lessons to teach me about what mattered and about *who* mattered more.

***A Quiet Reflection:** Although I would not wish the lowness I felt on that floor on anyone, it stands as proof that sometimes our lowest moments have the most to teach us.*

That loss was a very reflective moment in time for me. It forced me to go back and take a long, hard look at myself. It was cathartic because it forced me to release what was no longer mine and get my act together.

What felt like my own fall from grace was, in fact, a shedding of the self I'd become comfortable with—a self that was not my best. I realized I had more to offer the world than that version of me. But I may have never known it if I hadn't hit the floor.

That floor did not define me. That low moment forced me to pick myself up. When I did, my confidence level grew because I had nothing to lose. I committed to making something of myself no matter what.

So, I did.

That floor did not break me—it revealed me. It gave me the part of myself I'd stopped listening to.

***For The Reader:** When something threatens to break you, you have a choice. A choice to pick yourself up or let yourself stay beaten down. It's your choice and only your choice.*

Within that choice, there is a second opportunity for growth. You get to choose how you pick yourself up and where you go from there.

Choose to rise from the floor so that you get to meet the version of yourself waiting on the other side of it. That is the lesson I share with you.

But I cannot make the choice for you. It is yours to finish. It is your response to adversity that determines the outcome.

We're all told that shit happens; it's what you do from there that is important.

Don't be afraid to reinvent yourself, this time, any time, many times. There is no limit. You set the rules.

Chapter Seven

The Map Wasn't Just Mine Anymore

"When it all came apart, I didn't break. I adjusted."
—Bill

I Knew Her Before I Knew Her

Looking back, I wish I had a big family. I wish that I had six or seven children running around the house and that I got to watch them grow older and take on the world themselves. Those bachelor years were a lot of fun, but they didn't build anything lasting. I learned a great deal about myself during those years, but ultimately, they are just echoes of a time gone by. Echoes of, "Sure, if I only knew then what I know now."

I don't know how long I would have stayed a bachelor, stayed on that course if Milissa, in her '80s aerobics outfit, bouncing black curls, and open heart, hadn't snared me in the racquetball club that day. Perhaps forever. Maybe I'd be 75 and single and haunted by a deeper regret for not having the family I secretly dreamt of. A dream so sacred, I could scarcely admit it even to myself.

I'll never know what my life would have looked like without her, because my course was forever changed the moment she walked into the BQE Racquetball Club and I heard her name. "I'm Milissa."

In that very same moment, fresh off the court from a winning racquetball game, I proclaimed to my friends, "I'm going to marry that woman." They laughed. But I meant it.

Even though something deep inside me knew that my path led to her, it was not a straight or easy line to get to where we are now—retired in our beautiful home, watching our wonderful daughter chart her own course.

Our path started like this.

Frankie and Ray urged me to get back on the court, "Come on, man. Stop staring at her. You have enough girls. Let's play." I tried, but I was too distracted. I simply couldn't play another game until I met her. I couldn't let her walk out the door without first introducing myself. I needed her to know that I saw her.

Milissa walked to the other side of the club where the restaurant sat. I had no intentions of being pushy or too forward; I just wanted an introduction. Even if nothing came of it, I would know I tried. So, I walked straight up to her and said,

"Hi, my name is Bill. I play here regularly. I hear you're interviewing with Bill Louie?"

She smiled at me, light and open, "Yes, I am. How'd you know that?"

"I try to keep an eye on important things that go on here," I replied, matching her easy smile.

That was enough for this moment. I didn't want to overdo it; I just wanted her to know my name and make the introduction. "I just wanted to welcome you and wish you luck," I said as I turned to leave. "Oh, and if Bill Louie has any brains, he'd hire you in a minute."

"He did," she replied. "I start on Monday."

Silent joy overwhelmed me.

Kismet

For a while, that was it.

I saw Milissa regularly, since I was at the club playing racquetball five days a week, and she was teaching class almost every day. I learned more about her. She was an aerobics teacher at six or seven different clubs. She was also a language teacher in a high school nearby, teaching a few different languages. She was a hustler, just like me—trying to make a couple bucks here, a couple bucks there. And she had the skill to prove it.

We were kindred spirits.

One day, I worked up the nerve to take her class. I remember it well. My towel was slung around my neck, and she came over to say hi to me after a game. I said, "I'm thinking of doing your aerobics class today. Is it okay if I join?"

"Sure," she replied, "of course."

I secured my place in the back of her class. It was just me and about 40 women. At that time, I was the only guy brave enough to join. Months later, other guys started coming too.

During that class, I followed her instruction, kicking my leg up high in that '80s aerobics style, moving with the music, and getting much more winded than I'd like to admit. She walked around the class and gave little corrections to form and pace. Every time she neared, I intentionally made a small mistake so she'd come over to correct me, and we'd get a small, fleeting moment together.

We were friendly, but I never pushed it beyond that. I was content to take my time and let things unfold naturally. I wanted us to be as much her choice as mine.

One day after a game, I noticed her sitting at a table in the restaurant all by herself, and I walked right up to her and said, "Hey, Milissa. Someday, would you like to go out to lunch?" I anticipated her saying no or holding me off, but either way, I would respect her choice.

Instead, she smiled up at me and asked, "Where do you want to go?"

Wow! See what happens if you just ask!

Our first date wasn't someday; it was *that day*. That in itself said something to me.

We decided on a small Chinese restaurant about five miles away from the club. She got in my car, and I drove us down. It was the middle of the day, after lunchtime and before dinner, and there was nobody in the restaurant except for us.

We ordered one of everything on the menu, and we laughed and had good food and an even better conversation. It was wonderful, more than just surface level. It was easy, natural. I could relate to her, and I suspected the feeling was mutual. She got me in a way that nobody else ever had, and I knew I would do anything to be with her and to be seen like that for the rest of my life.

But I also knew that I wasn't the man she deserved. Not yet. First, I had to shape up.

Patience, Bill, Patience

We didn't go on another date for a year.

Not because I didn't want to. Not because my conviction changed. But because Bill, "The Bachelor," wasn't who Milissa deserved. I was determined to go wherever I had to go to pull my shit together. To do whatever I had to do. My strength of mind and pure determination propelled me forward.

I knew I had to be single, truly single, with no one besides myself to keep me company before I could be ready for the true and lasting relationship I hoped to have with Milissa. So, I broke off the numerous casual relationships I was in at the time with a finality that my friends and girlfriends rebelled against. A lot of the women I was seeing had grown attached to me, attached to the wild lifestyle and the company I gave them. With a lot of them, I had distanced myself in the past, attempting to move forward, but never committing to it.

Naturally, they thought this was just another beat along the same course.

But this time I meant it. I was done. I had found something different, something *more*.

Once I made the choice, the decision, there was no looking back. Once I put my mind to something, I accomplish it. I do not leave room for doubt, only action. Forward. Always forward. In love, in business, in whatever I set out to do. This is how I move, how I navigate the world and whatever challenges it asks me to stand up and meet.

Admittedly, it surprised me how different it was with Milissa. The resolve I had that it was her, only her. And the lifestyle changes I was willing to make because of it. I left no room for doubt.

It forced me to reflect and to look back at my first marriage to Susan and my second marriage to Gina. I could see how that second marriage, especially, was one of convenience and one at safe, arms-length distance so I wouldn't wind up shattered, back on that floor like I had been when Susan and I ended.

Map the Scars, Chart the Stars

It got me thinking about my divorce from Susan. And how during this time, Carmine and I sold the C&B Fruit Hut, and my career took a stark pivot. I needed a change after our relationship crumbled overnight. I needed to pick myself up off the metaphorical floor and rewrite my story.

Both of Susan's brothers had been NYC cops, passing their entrance exams with near perfect scores. Her father constantly boasted, placed so much value on his sons and their careers, and repeatedly told me I could never make it as a cop. I was not like them.

Because I'm the kind of guy who doesn't like to be told I can't do something, I took those tests after Susan and I split. His sons might have gotten near perfect scores, but I did one better. Because I was a veteran, I got five extra points added to whatever score I got. And I got a 100. So I knew my 105 score would sting big time.

At the time, I was still angry, still carrying the unhealed wound of being underestimated. Seeing myself as the victim in Susan's and my story, I had to make sure her father knew that I had achieved what his sons hadn't. I mailed him my test scores in an envelope that had to be signed for, so that I knew he got it.

I was on the waiting list for about two years after I took those tests, but eventually, I became an officer. I met Gina in the New York Police Academy as a rookie, and we quickly fell into an easy friendship. She was a cop by day and a Playboy bunny by night—not the Playboy Magazine bunny. She was a bunny waitress in the Playboy Club in Manhattan—a complete dichotomy, being both one thing and another.

Having already had quite a varied life and career myself, I could relate.

Gina was one of the nicest people I've ever met. I still stand by that statement to this day. She started staying over at my place night after night. Being rookies, that kind of relationship was frowned upon; you needed to be married. So, instead of continuing to sneak around, we got hitched.

It was a courthouse marriage, fast and simple, so we had the piece of paper to prove it and could continue our easy relationship for however long we wanted. It was a marriage of convenience, but it was also exactly what I needed at the time. After three years, I could feel myself pulling away, getting bored. Not from Gina's company, but because our relationship lacked the mental stimulation I craved.

Unlike Susan, we didn't end with screaming voices and slamming doors. We didn't end with me back on that floor, wondering how in the hell I got here. No, with Gina, it was a mutual parting—a natural stopping point.

One day, she moved out, and that was it. We met each other a couple of times for lunch or dinner during the months that followed, but never anything romantic. Just old friends reuniting. When she met a new guy she loved, I was happy for her.

And for me? I was more than happy to be "The Bachelor".

Carousel Horses

I reflected back on my parting with both Susan and Gina during the days I worked to get my life on track to become a man worthy of Milissa. For perhaps the very first time, I took accountability: for my role in the relationship, for the things I did too much of, and for the things I didn't do enough of. I realized that accountability is what was missing in the past. It's what I wasn't willing to acknowledge during my bachelor years.

But a man of accountability is what Milissa deserved.

It took me almost a year to shed all that wasn't serving me and then build a solid foundation on top of what was. During the time that passed, Milissa remained at the forefront of my mind, and I navigated the world with unfettered trust that if we were meant to work out, the timing would as well.

Almost a year to the day after our first date, I walked toward the entrance to the racquetball club. The adjoining restaurant had a big window that opened to the outside. As I walked past, movement in that window caught my eye. I saw Milissa sitting there with some other guy, her head thrown back in laughter.

Call it what you like, but again, she caught my eye.

That did it for me.

I knew it was time to stop working to be better and trust that in that moment, I was already enough for her. I knew if I didn't make my move, I would lose her to this man in the window or to someone else.

That was the day I decided, now or never.

The very next day, I waited for her class to clear out. Only when we were alone did I walk up to her. "Would you like to go out to dinner with me in Manhattan? I know a lot of very nice places."

Her reply was instant and easy, as if she'd been waiting all these months for me to ask her this very question, "A friend of mine told me about the carousel horses that are being displayed as an exhibition in Manhattan. How do you feel about horses?"

"Oh, I love them. That's great," I replied. The fact is, if she asked me to go see bacteria, I would have given the same answer!

"How about Friday?" she replied.

"Friday's great. I'll come pick you up."

We drove into the city and went to see the carousel horses that were on exhibition in the lobby of this big, beautiful building. Then we went to a comedy club and later had dinner at a fabulous restaurant. We walked and walked, talking the whole time, until 2:00 a.m.

If it were up to me, we'd still be walking.

Carousels were the theme of our wedding a year or so later. We had little carousels on every table to remind us of that date. Carousels were on our invitations, wedding decor, and anywhere that could remind us of that wonderful evening. Our wedding was incredible. We had a famous band—The Impalas—play. Everyone stayed on the dance floor all night long. It was the best day of my life.

I was not the same boy who watched with hesitation and doubt as Susan walked down the aisle in her frilly white dress. I was not the person in that courthouse with Gina, marrying for a piece of paper and simple companionship.

I was a man who was ready for lasting love—a man who looked upon Milissa walking down the aisle with a deep knowing that I had found my partner, my equal.

A Quiet Reflection: *Milissa is the woman who has challenged me endlessly over the past 40 years and counting. She's my best friend. She's admirable, extremely intelligent, highly successful, very independent…and sometimes, just sometimes, the biggest pain in my ass. I respect her highly.*

My path in life has been made so much brighter and bolder because of her.

Reflecting back now, I see that I didn't fail at love. I was just young, and I hadn't become the man yet who would succeed at it.

I matured. I grew up. I found someone who called me out and who changed who I wanted to be not because she forced me, but because I wanted to. She continues to keep me in my place and silently demands the respect she deserves.

To this day, I'm an incredibly independent guy. But I've learned about real relationships, real sharing, and the real meaning of the journey.

There is no greater pride than when I embrace what I learn from her and become someone better because of it. Yes, of course, we argue from time to time. We're human. But our love and respect for each other always supports our relationship.

For The Reader: *We all want to learn. We want to stay open. We just want to grow into something more than we were yesterday.*

*But the truth is—**we don't know what we don't know.***

Not until life shows us. Not until we stumble. Not until we get knocked down and have the guts to get back up.

It's only after we've made the mistake, only after we've felt the sting, that we can look back and say, **"I'll try not to do that again."**

So let me share with you one of the most important analogies I've ever carried:

"In life, I use all of my erasers, but I try not to erase in the same place more than once."

I've made mistakes. Plenty. I've earned every scar. I'm tougher now. More ready. Prepared.

It means I've stopped punishing myself for being human. It means I've started honoring the lessons hidden inside every misstep. It means I've stopped chasing perfection—and started chasing **growth.**

I encourage you to do the same. Because if you're not learning, you're not living.

Act Three

Reflection & Reinvention

Chapter Eight

The Compass I Became

"I didn't climb to escape the bottom. I climbed to understand it. And every time I fell, I carried something back up with me. That's how I built my life—layer by layer, truth by truth."

—Bill

I Used to Think Golf was for Old Men

There's something about stepping onto the golf course at 5:00 a.m. when nobody's there and the rest of the world is sleeping. The sun peaks over the horizon, the birds sing their morning song, and deer bound across the dewy morning grass. It's peaceful. It's meditative. It's the perfect place for a thinker like me.

I played racquetball for decades, and I was good. The game took me to far-reaching corners of the world, playing semi-professionally, simply for the love and joy of it. It was not my career, not something I pursued for any sense of success—aside from the satisfaction of a winning game. If you asked me at the time, at 25 years old, if I'd ever take up golf, I would have laughed in your face and told you that golf was for old men.

Now that I am indeed older, wiser, and have lived a full life, I wish I'd picked up golf far sooner, because I know now that it has so much to teach us about life. Golf makes you think. It forces you to reflect on a bad shot. When you're frustrated and taking your shot from the place of *I'm going to kill that ball,* you realize it only makes things worse. I've come to realize that I can yell and scream at that tiny white ball all I want, but it's not going to do anything. It's not going to change the trajectory of the swing I already took.

Just like with that little golf ball, you become less and less satisfied with the flow of your life when you put too much pressure on controlling the trajectory of where you're going. That pressure is not going to give you back control. It is only going to strip away your satisfaction and warp your perspective of what the journey truly means.

For me, my unrelenting pursuit of career success and seeking control waned as I crested 60. It was only as I dipped my toe into semi-retirement that I was finally willing to slow down, pick up a golf club, and learn all the sport had to teach me. I was finally ready to move not in pursuit, but in joy.

You can learn a lot from joy. Joy doesn't demand achievement. It invites presence.

As I walk onto that quiet golf course each morning, my heart fills with joy; it gives me space to think and time to reflect back on the journey, and on my career trajectory. I had 17 jobs across almost as many different fields: shoeshiner; laboratory technologist; brick layer; house painter; owner of a fruit & vegetable store, a trucking and distribution business, a catering store, and an importing & exporting business; general manager of an ice cream manufacturer; vice president of a specialty desserts company and of a furniture and design business; and senior business consultant for some of the largest aerospace and defense contractors in the world. The list goes on.

I found success in them all. But I also found lessons, many lessons about life.

This might seem baffling to those who have stayed with a single company for more than 40 years. But for me, it makes perfect sense. I wouldn't change a single moment of it—not the incredible financial and career success I found time and time again or the inevitable losses and lessons that naturally came along with it.

I've come to see that financial success is the only metric some people measure themselves by. After all, it's what the system, what society, tells us to do—to judge how good our lives are by the numbers in our bank accounts. That's why some people stay on the path laid out in front of them, because it feels like the safest way to ensure that metric stays intact.

For me, I'm more comfortable stepping off the path and following my own internal compass instead. I frequently challenge systems that place value on output rather than inherent dignity. I always have, and I always will. I know that the value of life lies not in the same path that everyone is walking, but within the footsteps you take off the path.

The value is on the roads you decide to walk all on your own.

It is for this reason that I have a very different relationship with money—the metric society asks us to measure ourselves by. From the days of boyhood, I pulled myself and my family up from nothing to something by the skin of my teeth: saving pennies, shining shoes, and working three jobs at the age of 8. In adulthood, I started businesses, built them up to more success than I ever could have imagined, and then lost them because of forces outside my control.

These trials might have taught me to seek money and to define myself by the number. Instead, they taught me one core thing—*I know how to make money.* And because I have had unfettered proof since the young age of 7 that I knew how to make it, throughout the course of my life, it never mattered how many times I lost it.

Because I knew it would always return to me.

I carried this quiet knowing with me throughout my career. Every time I "lost" financial success when a business endeavor failed, when the mafia forced my hand, when the politics of governments caused the millions of dollars I was promised to suddenly disappear—I saw these periods not as failure, but as pure *opportunity*.

It was an opportunity to start fresh, follow the thread of interest that tugged at me, and build back something better. Instead of defining myself by the numbers, I moved throughout my life following my internal compass. It never led me astray. I moved with truth, self-honesty, and acceptance over perfection.

Most of all, I *moved.*

Momentum Builds on the Road Less-Traveled

With the voice of Susan's narcissistic father always in my ear—
"You will never be a NYC cop like my two sons. You don't have
what it takes."—picking myself up off that barren floor was
brutal.

It was 1973, and I was still recovering from my divorce. The
small fruit and vegetable business I opened with Carmine
three years back was booming. Selling over 1,000 pounds of
fish, fruit, and vegetables every week, we were the talk of the
neighborhood, and money was good. Carmine and I built
a successful business over three short years, earning a great
living from our shop. But just like that boy of 7 who thrived
when he was always moving, always striving, holding down
multiple jobs and going to school—one business wasn't enough
for me at 23 years old either.

"You don't have what it takes," reverberated through my mind.
But I knew that I did. My test score of 105 to become a NYC
cop proved it. My heart proved it. I was so much more than
just that hustling kid from Brooklyn, and I was determined to
make a difference. Not only for me and for my family, but for
my community.

So when I finally got called off the waitlist and onto the police
force as a rookie, I didn't hesitate; I jumped at the chance to be
a NYC cop. At the chance to play my part in making the streets
and neighborhoods safer. It didn't matter that I also had the
C&B Fruit Hut to run with Carmine. I knew I didn't have to be
one thing or the other. I knew that if I chose to do so, I could
be both.

That's exactly what I did.

I am forever grateful to myself for not falling into step with what society expected of me and for taking my own path down a far less-traveled road instead. Whenever an opportunity presented itself, if it interested me, like becoming a cop did, I took it.

If it didn't, I let it pass me by.

I never thought I had to do it all. I just didn't fall into the trap of thinking that I could only do, or be, one thing forever. By 23, I had lived the lives of many different people. I was the newspaper delivery boy. The lab technologist. The conscientious objector standing up for my country in Vietnam. The recently returned-home veteran who started a business with a friend from the neighborhood. A husband. A NYC cop. And a man who was ready to try something new.

As soon as I felt that nudge, telling me something new and different was on the horizon, sure enough, an opportunity presented itself.

Fate had Other Plans

A half a million dollars in cash was an astronomical sum in the '70s, worth over three million today. That's what they offered on the spot. Five Koreans in well-tailored suits stood in our tiny fruit shop one bright, sunny day in 1973, assessing it with satisfaction. "We want to buy your business," one of them announced.

Carmine and I were working together at the C&B Fruit Hut when these five men entered with the opportunity. We were deep in our routine of chatting with regulars, frying up fish sandwiches and loading up bag after bag of fresh fruit until a group of unfamiliar faces stepped into the store, cash in hand, and made us the offer we couldn't refuse.

They were prepared to act fast, and Carmine and I knew an incredible opportunity when we saw one. Even after splitting it between the two of us, half a million was still a fortune, especially for a couple of young guys in their early 20s. The decision was easy.

We took the deal—and in that instant, everything changed.

As part of the deal to sell our shop, we got to keep our truck—the same truck we used to haul food from the markets to stock our fruit and vegetable store. That truck would soon become the foundation of our next venture.

Carmine and I enjoyed working together, and we were good at it. Even though that small fruit hut was no longer ours, we assumed we'd simply buy another store nearby and continue the same routine—hitting the fish market at 2:00 a.m., loading up the truck, and distributing fresh produce to loyal customers each day.

But fate had other plans.

At the time, Carmine's brother was working for E.J. Korvettes, a chain of American discount department stores that eventually shut down in 1980. We'll circle back to the company shuttering its doors later. For now, what matters is that Carmine's brother was doing well, making deliveries for E.J. Korvettes with a truck of his own.

He offered to introduce us to the decision-makers at E.J. Korvettes just a few short weeks after selling our shop. Since we already had our own truck, Carmine turned to me and asked, "Bill, what do you think? Want to partner with me and use the truck to make deliveries like my brother?"

My response was a little unconventional, but that was typical for me. Instead of just saying yes, I listened to my internal compass and asked, "What if we buy your brother out, take over his truck, and build a distribution business for ourselves?"

I didn't have experience in this type of business. But I trusted my abilities, and I trusted Carmine. I knew we'd thrive if we put everything we had into it. And as it turned out, Carmine's brother was ready to retire anyway.

His terms were simple: "You have to buy me out."

I nodded my head and asked, "Alright, how much?"

"A quarter million," he replied.

Carmine and I weighed the decision carefully, but neither of us balked at the number. Using some of our money from the sale of our shop, we could afford it. We agreed, and before long, found ourselves not in the fruit and vegetable business—but in the trucking and distribution business.

Within weeks, E.J. Korvettes brought us on directly. We secured the account by sheer determination, selling them on who we were and what we could deliver. We sold them on our experience in business and our ability to build from scratch.

With that, Caputo Trucking LLC was born—not from expertise, but from belief in our ability to figure it out.

At the time, E.J. Korvettes operated 21 stores across the tristate area, and Carmine's brother had handled deliveries for three of them, which we then took on. But three wasn't enough for us. We started with those three stores, then quickly expanded to six, eight, and eventually to 12. We hired everyone we knew— my family, my brother, all his friends, and all of mine. Before long, we were managing store transfers, vendor returns, and home deliveries across most of the metropolitan area.

At the same time, I was navigating a second divorce. Gina and I ended our two-year marriage, and although it was amicable, it still stung. It still felt like a loss, like it defined me as a man. At the time, I wasn't interested in what the end of the marriage meant, so I poured everything I had into growing the trucking business. I worked tirelessly—17 hours a day, seven days a week. It was grueling, but it was necessary to reach the next level.

The effort paid off.

Business was thriving. Because of this, I felt secure enough in what Carmine and I had built to take a vacation. I needed to get away to set my mind right. I needed a change, a quiet place to think, reflect, and recalibrate, and I remembered some of my favorite customers back at C&B Fruit Hut who had told me about the magic of Machu Picchu in Peru. "You have to go, Bill. You just have to." Holding steadfast to their advice, I booked myself a solo trip down to South America.

A Journey of Becoming

I'm going to die, I'm going to die, I'm going to die. The thought kept coming at me the faster we traveled along the cliffside of the famed mountains in Peru, my mind flashing back to the vehicles we had passed on the train ride up the mountain, smashed and broken after falling off the cliffside.

Earlier that day, I boarded an old steam train to make the journey up to the ruins of Machu Picchu. That day, I was to finally set my eyes on the Incan citadel nestled atop the mountain ridge in the Peruvian Andes. The train slowly ascended the mountain, weaving back and forth, back and forth, across the width of the difficult terrain to make the climb.

While on board, precariously chugging along the cliffside, I wondered if this old steam train was even going to make it to the top. I wondered, that is, until it chugged to a stop and we were instructed to disembark. Not yet at the summit, the other passengers and I climbed into an old van to make the rest of the ascent.

We drove on a narrow, winding road, wide enough only for a single van. Every time we encountered another van coming down, the drivers launched into a staring match of who was going to back up and give way. When my driver lost, he didn't back up slowly or carefully. No, when it was our turn, the van picked up speed, accelerating in reverse, the tires balancing precariously on the cliff edge. My head filled with *I'm going to die, I'm going to die, I'm going to die.* But my heart relished in the journey.

When we finally reached the top, the ruins, the view, the *feeling*—they were indescribable. At that moment, almost 50 years ago, Machu Picchu was the most mystical place I'd ever been. I can confidently say, it still is to this day. I know anyone who has been there will agree—it's tranquil, breathtaking, and powerful.

Sitting there at the top of an incredible mountain, 7,972 feet above sea level, surrounded by other mountaintops over 10,000 feet, it feels like you're in the middle of the sky. It feels like you're close to heaven.

I did that trip up the mountain three times, on three different trips to Peru. Each time, I felt a little more comfortable with the journey to the top. Each time, I reflected on my own journey of coming from nothing and *becoming* someone I was proud of.

Each time I made it to the summit, I found the same little secluded area, looked out at the breathtaking view, and fell into a meditative state. Entranced by the mystical place, creative thoughts and opportunities simply seemed to find their way to me in Peru, anytime I slowed down enough to listen. *It wasn't just inspiration I found—it was an invitation.*

A Quiet Reflection: I used to think golf was for old men. Then I got old...and finally understood.

I didn't pick up the game out of ambition. I picked it up out of curiosity—and stayed because something about it kept speaking back. Not loudly, not obviously. But in the space between shots, somewhere between the silence and the swing.

It turns out, golf isn't about taking lessons. It's about learning them. That's what life is about, too.

For The Reader: *I'd love to share with you now, a few subtle, hard-earned truths I've learned that echo far beyond the fairways. Like my Billisms, here are ten truths to live by—even if you've never picked up a golf club.*

1. *If you're thinking about missing, you're already halfway there.* **Fear doesn't guide; it paralyzes.**

2. *Eighty percent of missed putts don't even reach the hole.* **Give it more, always a little more than you think.**

3. *The shot you're taking now has nothing to do with the one you just missed.* **Regret is heavy; carry less of it.**

4. *It's a tiny ball, and it never listens—so stop yelling at it.* **Some things just don't bend to your will. Breathe anyway.**

5. *Savor the day and the company; that's the real win.* **Everything else is just scorekeeping.**

6. *There's always tomorrow—***until there isn't. So let the gratitude linger, and play today like it counts.**

7. *Aim for the fence, not over it.* **Ambition is noble; wisdom knows when to pull back.**

8. *That extra yard? It just cost you 60.* **Sometimes the cost of "more" is everything you already had.**

9. *Practice doesn't make perfect—just better.* **But better is a good place to be.**

10. *Imagine where everyone else is.* **You're playing your own game, and you're already ahead. Stay present.**

Remember, as Wayne Gretzky originally said, "You miss 100% of the shots you don't take."

Life won't wait forever. Swing.

Chapter Nine

Every Fall is a Lesson, Every Chapter a Chance

"I didn't plan for what defined me."
–Bill

The Architecture of Building Something More

Although the success of my trucking business with Carmine is what allowed me to travel to Peru for the first time, soon my jet-setting trips back and forth to the beautiful country wouldn't be on my own dime, not after opportunity found me. Little did I know that an alpaca rug and a series of seemingly disconnected, yet fateful events would lead me to my next great peak.

On that first trip, and for many after, I stayed at the Gran Hotel Bolivar in Lima, Peru—a five-star luxury resort that rose six stories above the Lima skyline and hosted many high-profile guests. With unparalleled service, they treated me like a king and served up some of the most delicious food to ever hit my lips.

Just down the block from the hotel was a store that sold beautiful alpaca rugs in all different colors. Walking along the street, I caught sight of the luxurious fabric that beckoned me inside. On the wall in the shop was a stunning rug that stood out among the rest.

At the time, I traveled with a guide, a wonderful woman from Colombia who served as my translator until I could pick up the language for myself. She accompanied me inside this tiny shop, and with my eyes alight on the rug, I asked her to inquire how much it would cost to take it home with me.

She returned with a figure in Peruvian sol. Translated to American dollars, it would run me $90.

Only $90? It couldn't be.

"No, this one right here." I pointed to the woven art piece hanging from the wall. I knew enough to know that a rug of this caliber was worth far, far more.

"Yes, this one. It's $90," she replied with a mirthful smile at my wonder. "The rest of the rugs are even less."

"In that case," I said, "I'll take four."

That day, I bought the ornate alpaca rug and three others, all of varying colors. When I returned home to Brooklyn, I hung the grandest one from my own wall as an art piece for my guests to admire when they came to visit.

Admire it, they did.

A few months later, as I walked down the Manhattan streets, in between deliveries for E.J. Korvettes, I spotted a similar alpaca rug sitting underneath a coffee table. This one was displayed in an upscale interior decor shop in NYC. Curious, I walked inside to admire it. Then I saw the price tag—$4,600.

It was black and white, and although it was 100% alpaca hair, compared to the varied hues of my own rug, it honestly looked like a piece of shit. But it sold at a premium in NYC.

The store owner wandered over to where I was inspecting the rug, "Hello, sir. Can I help you?"

"Yeah. Do you have any other alpaca rugs?" I replied, my curiosity piquing.

"Oh, no. This is it. I would love to have more, but I can't get them. I wish I could."

A thread of opportunity tugged at me then.

I nodded my head but didn't say more. Instead, I went straight home, took my own rug off the wall, and carefully wrapped it up. Then I drove over the Brooklyn Bridge back into Manhattan with the rug carefully nestled in the back seat. Parking along the curb outside that same interior design shop, I carried my rug inside and walked straight up to the man I had spoken with before.

"I have this alpaca rug and three others—and I can buy *many* more for you."

He pulled the rug out of its packaging, and I could see his excitement bubbling as he admired the detail. He called the other salespeople out from the back. "Take a look at this. Look at how gorgeous this is. How soft. How colorful." They all nodded in agreement as the quality of my $90 rug far outpaced the one they were selling for $4,600.

Turning back to me, he asked, "How much is it?"

"This one's $3,000," I replied easily, "But there are other ones I can get that are a little cheaper."

He stared back at me, wide-eyed. "Can you really get me more of these? At that price?"

"Absolutely. How many do you want?"

He set me up with an order of 16 rugs to start with, and that gave me a reason to go back to Peru. I saw a real opportunity here to turn a profit. My mind whirred: If I flew down to Peru, bought 16 rugs for about $60 a piece, shipped them back to the US, and sold them to this NYC interior design shop for $3,000 a pop—the margin was incredible, and my heart sang at getting to return to Peru. This time, I wasn't going for pleasure. This time, I had business to attend to…and an opportunity to garner even *more*.

It's important to mention that a few years before this moment, one of my customers at C&B Fruit Hut was a stockbroker. She came to me one day and casually asked, "Bill, do you ever invest in stocks?" At the time, I didn't think I had enough money to invest in the stock market, but she promised me she had an opportunity for me, so I bought in. She turned the $6,000 I gave her into $18,000 in three months, investing it in the new premium television service, HBO. Thinking I made out like a bandit with the purest gold, I foolishly sold the stock a few months later. Had I held onto it, it would be worth many times that amount today.

Needless to say, this woman had my trust.

So when she heard about the opportunity I had with the alpaca rugs, she suggested I meet two of her colleagues, venture capitalists, who might be interested in investing in me should I want to make this alpaca opportunity a tried-and-true importing and exporting business. "You're the kind of entrepreneur they would be willing to support, Bill. You're the guy."

Never one to shy away from building something new, I jumped at the chance.

Just like Carmine and I sold E.J. Korvettes on giving us an account based on our business prowess alone, the same thing happened here. I met with the two prominent men in Manhattan and sold them on *me*. One was an original owner of McDonald's, and the other made steel dumpsters for every business in America. They had the funds to contribute and jumped at the chance to invest in me. These two men became my business partners in my new venture, Charter Merchants International.

Together, we opened up a small office in Port Jefferson on Long Island and incorporated the business. Within a few months, I was flying back and forth from NYC to Peru on their dime, exporting not just handwoven alpaca rugs but Cadillac™ limousines, range hoods, stoves, tile, toilet bowls, sinks…the list went on. All of the items were exported exclusively through Peru.

I split my time between running Caputo Trucking with Carmine in NY and flying down to Peru to grow Charter Merchants International. For a few years, life felt like a dream. *But dreams, like markets, shift with the wind.*

I was in my 'Bachelor' era, jet-setting back and forth to South America and running two flourishing businesses. Grateful for it all, and high on life, I felt like I couldn't be touched.

But like the fable of Icarus, who flew too close to the sun, there is no place for hubris, pride, or arrogance in business. There are too many things outside of one man's control, and you don't always get to decide how high you fly; the threat of it all coming crashing down is ever-present.

Climbing From the Ashes

Life dealt me many coincidences and opportunities in Peru— from running into an old friend at the First National Bank of Peru while I was setting up my accounts, who had married a Peruvian woman and was now working as the president of the bank that I used to run my business to the Man in the Mountain, an American aristocrat from Boston, who bought himself an entire mountain and welcomed people all around the world to discuss philosophy, including me. I got to engage with brilliant minds from all different backgrounds on that mountain.

It all gave me hope for the future. It felt like I was *meant* to be in Peru; how could I not keep climbing?

One night over dinner back in Brooklyn, my father, my younger brother, and I were chatting about my new importing and exporting venture. My father, long returned from Florida, was now living in Queens. He said, "You know, my super in my apartment building, his brother is Peruvian. He's supposedly a big guy in Peru, with a real prominent position. I can ask him to introduce you."

As it turns out, this brother was a commanding general in the Peruvian army who specialized in procurement. A few days later, the meeting was set, and another opportunity landed in my lap.

Waiting in the lobby of the Bolivar Hotel in Peru, one of the smartly dressed bellboys came up to me, "Sir, General Ariste's driver is here for you." I walked outside to a sleek, chauffeured car. The driver opened the door, and I slid inside, coming face-to-face with the general waiting for me on the plush leather seats. My father's landlord's brother—General Ariste—sat there in regular clothes, casual, yet still imposing. His uniform was nowhere to be seen. "What do you think of horses?" he said in greeting. "Do you like watching the horses?"

He owned seven different horses that were racing that evening at the racetrack, so that's where we went. It was the most lavish, gorgeous racetrack I have ever seen in my entire life. We sat in his box upstairs, located flush with the finish line, and made our bets. Then, General Ariste snapped his fingers, and dinner and drinks were served to us on actual silver platters.

Two of his seven horses won that night; the other five lost. He was impressed that I picked his winners. I didn't bet on any other horses besides his. I picked only the two winners that night.

"You know, Bill," he said casually after a winning race, impressed by my picks, "One of the things Peru is known for is its coffee. Peruvian coffee is famous for its flavor and quality because of how it's grown. I know a lot of different people. I'll introduce you to the farm cooperative. Get to know them; make them a deal."

He made the introduction, nothing more. But that was all I needed.

I met with the president of the farm cooperative, and within a week, Charter Merchants International had a contract to buy three million pounds of coffee per year. That was just the starting figure. If things went well, we planned to scale up to ten million.

Separately, my partners secured a deal with Liberty Coffee Company in New York. I bought the coffee in Peru for $.60 per pound. We sold it to Liberty for $1.69 per pound.

At first, I thought the margin was just a few pennies. What could that possibly amount to?

My partner smiled.

"$1.08," he said, "Times ten million pounds."

That's when I did the math.

Ten million pounds. One dollar and eight cents of profit per pound.

$10.8 million.

It wasn't pennies. It was scale. And it was ours.

Flying high, there was talk of my hiring a butler or a chauffeur. At only 30 years old, I thought I was set—set for life, until, out of the blue, I got a phone call from General Aristes's secretary. "Bill, we have a problem."

After a successful coup d'état in 1980, the Armed Forces of Peru overthrew the dictatorship regime that had been in power for over a decade. The country shifted key economic policies, including new rules for exports. They introduced export taxes to increase their competitiveness in the foreign trade market.

For me, the effect of this regime change was sudden, harsh, and devastating.

For anything leaving Peru, the government now set the price. The farm cooperative had no choice but to change its contract with me to adhere to these new policies. "I'm so sorry, Bill, but we can only sell you the coffee for $1.69 a pound."

The very same number, I had agreed upon with the Liberty Coffee Company.

With our profit margins now nonexistent, my partners came to me urgently and matter-of-factly said, "We need to demolish the business. We're pulling our funding. You have to close Charter Merchants, Bill. There's no other option." I saw then that they were only in this business to make money. As soon as it became clear that the opportunity had disappeared, their investment in me disappeared too.

Just as swiftly, the Liberty Coffee Company served me a $2.5 million lawsuit. They had been promised 3 million pounds of coffee, and I could no longer deliver. Still just a young guy, I had no idea how to navigate this time in my life. I was scared. I thought I was going to jail when that lawsuit landed on my desk.

The only thing I knew for sure was that I had lost everything I had built. I did the only thing I could and followed the advice of my partners—overnight, I shuttered the doors of Charter Merchants International.

Everything fell apart as rapidly as it had come together. And when the dust settled, I was alone—with nothing but my name and my will.

The crash was lonely. Devastating. Confusing. And entirely outside of my control.

No More Asking Why, I Took Control

I had no choice but to pick myself up from the bottom…again. I had no choice but to move forward. In this instance, it was diversification that saved me. When one business crashed, I still had another to keep me afloat. To keep my head above water.

During the few years of running Charter Merchants International, I never left the trucking business behind. Carmine and I had grown it to the point where we didn't need to physically make any deliveries ourselves. Our team, made up of friends and family, did the work; we ran the business and issued the paychecks. When Liberty Coffee Company served me that lawsuit, I cut my losses and returned full-time to Caputo Trucking with Carmine.

If I could no longer grow my importing and exporting business, I would grow this one instead.

I set my mind to this new goal and began poring over paper after paper, analyzing every aspect of the business to identify the best opportunities for growth. What I found was unexpected and sparked the same out of control feeling in me that losing everything with Charter Merchants International had.

Carmine's girlfriend, Jamie, was stealing from the business.

Jamie went to school for accounting, so just like we hired other friends and family, we had brought Jamie on to do our books a few years back. The moment I uncovered proof that she had been embezzling money for months, my heart leaped into my throat. I felt taken advantage of. Fury rose in my chest. But unlike with Charter Merchants International, where I had no control over the outcome, righting this wrong *was* within my control.

I took action immediately and confronted Carmine. I showed him the receipts, the undeniable evidence that Jamie was stealing from him. From me. From *us*.

"I want her out, Carmine," I insisted. "We can't have people stealing; it could cripple our business. She's got to go." The worry that I was truly about to lose *everything* tugged at me, fueling my resolve.

Carmine, a habitual smoker, grew visibly anxious as I confronted him, puffing away at his cigarette faster than usual. He shook his head—he wouldn't do it. "Sorry, I can't, Bill. I won't." Jamie controlled their relationship, and Carmine was comfortable with the arrangement. No matter what she had done, he refused to push her out.

Even if it meant screwing us both over.

This situation put me in a tough spot. I couldn't just ignore the fact that I was being stolen from, but I had also built this company from the ground up and wasn't ready to walk away. I couldn't, not after Charter Merchants International had just crumbled before my eyes. I needed Caputo Trucking now more than ever.

I turned to my lawyers for advice. Their response was straightforward and unexpected: "Bill, Carmine's the Vice President. You're the President. Fire him."

Sure, Carmine is the one who'd originally come to me with the idea of getting into the trucking business. But I was the one willing to put in more effort and more capital. We both agreed on our positions early on, and I had held up my end of the bargain as President, even while running Charter Merchants International.

My role in the company gave me the authority to make tough decisions—including letting my friend go. I didn't want to do it. It felt heavy in my chest just to consider it. But I wasn't about to stand by while an employee was stealing from our business either. I knew exactly what needed to be done.

I didn't wait. I acted.

First, I fired Jamie. When Carmine refused to accept that, I fired him next. He still owned his shares in the company, so he wasn't walking away with nothing, but he was no longer an employee. He no longer had a say in running the business.

Going at it alone didn't intimidate me. I've always embraced opportunities and challenges without hesitation, so fear was not a factor. If I trusted myself to adapt and *build* from nothing, I could do this too. Losing a business? Losing a business partner? Those were simply new opportunities to grow.

And that's exactly what I did. I grew and grew that trucking business until forces beyond my control made me watch as it all came crashing down.

Adjustments, Not Absolutes

I put in the work every single day, and before I knew it, I had grown what Carmine and I built into something *more*—much more. I leased a fleet of 26 sleek Mercedes-Benz® trucks, serving all 21 E.J. Korvettes department stores. Business was booming, and with Jamie no longer siphoning money off the top, my earnings had never been better.

At the time, I was operating out of a small warehouse in Long Island City—one I acquired back when Carmine and I only had a couple of trucks. The routine for my employees was simple: pick up goods from the department store, bring them to the warehouse, load them onto the trucks, and send them out for delivery.

It wasn't long until the business outgrew that space. I needed a facility that could accommodate more than just a few trucks. And, as always, I wasn't afraid to scale. It was a bold move, but I took the leap.

I secured a larger warehouse in Greenpoint, a neighborhood in Brooklyn, equipped with eight loading bays and extensive racks, perfectly suited to accommodate the growing scale of my business. It was massive, and at $6,000 per month in 1970—equivalent to about $50,000 per month today—it was a significant investment.

But the business could sustain it.

At the time, E.J. Korvettes was by far my biggest client. They never missed a payment with me, although I had heard that wasn't the case with everyone they worked with. Still, I didn't dwell on it—I had 200 small accounts and two major ones: E.J. Korvettes and Safemart, an electronics retailer specializing in in-room hotel safes, along with stereo equipment, refrigerators, washing machines, and more.

Securing the Safemart account required a substantial investment in my business. Their insurance company mandated that I install alarms in the warehouse and on all my trucks. They also insisted that each vehicle be equipped with two-way radios. Since my fleet wasn't outfitted with that technology, I had to spend a considerable amount to meet their requirements.

I didn't hesitate. I made the investment without question.

I felt confident making such a large investment—Safemart was a major win, and with E.J. Korvettes alongside all my smaller accounts, my revenue far exceeded my overhead.

But life has a way of throwing curveballs, no matter how secure things seem. Only a few years after shuttering the doors of Charter Merchants International, I was in for another smackdown.

Installing the alarm systems set off a domino effect. A series of unexpected events unfolded, each hitting me harder than the last.

For five years, E.J. Korvettes always paid on time. But in our sixth year of doing business together, they went bankrupt—leaving me stuck with half a million dollars in unpaid invoices. Just like that, my biggest account was gone.

When I went to the bankruptcy court, they laid it out for me plainly: "Your #297 on the list. You'll likely get a penny per dollar." In other words, I could kiss that money goodbye—I was never getting it back.

I knew my revenue wouldn't be as high as before without my largest account as a safety net, but I wasn't too worried—I had savings in the business and other accounts and enough financial stability to keep going for a while.

Still, the setbacks didn't stop there.

Soon after, my massive warehouse was burglarized. It didn't take long for the police to track down the culprits—the same guys who had installed my alarm system. That's how they managed to break in so easily. As it turned out, they were part of a mafia crime family operating out of New York.

I was robbed by the mafia. Not by force. By familiarity. They knew the system because they built it.

The story was all over the papers, and from that moment on, I found myself under scrutiny. The next events came brutally and in quick succession.

When Safemart, now my largest client, learned that the break-in was linked to the mafia, they had a lot of questions. First, their insurance company called me in and required me to take a polygraph—a lie detector test. Then, I received a letter from their lawyer stating they wanted to press charges, suspecting that I might have been involved in the theft or had been stealing from the companies I worked with.

The irony wasn't lost on me—I had exposed Carmine's girlfriend for stealing, and now my most important client believed I was guilty of the same crime. The lie detector test became my one and only chance to clear my name and get out of a difficult situation.

I had no hesitation taking the polygraph—I knew I wasn't involved and welcomed the opportunity to prove it. I had no connections to the mafia; I had just hired some guy a friend recommended. How was I supposed to know? Plus, the burglary had hurt my business far more than it affected Safemart. I was prepared to make that clear. I was innocent, and I was ready to fight for myself.

But somehow…I failed the lie detector test.

At least, that's what the insurance company claimed. The fallacy of it all was that a test said I didn't tell the truth, when I knew that *I* had. I never saw the actual results, and even if I did, I wouldn't have known how to interpret them. There was no way to challenge their decision, no proof to dispute their claim. But I knew I was innocent. It all felt like a convenient excuse for them to cut ties.

The next day, Safemart called. "Bill, our insurance company won't allow us to continue doing business with you. We're done."

Just like that, my largest remaining account was gone.

Losing my two biggest accounts in just a few months made it impossible to keep the business afloat. My lawyers told me there was only one option: declare bankruptcy.

Seemingly overnight, I went from having plenty of money, running a thriving trucking business, and living the carefree bachelor's life to filing for bankruptcy.

Losing both Charter Merchants International and Caputo Trucking in the span of just a few years threatened to pull me under. It held up the mirror, showing me what kind of man I was when I had everything and what kind of man I was when I had nothing.

The face staring back at me did not change. Because the rise and fall, the winning and losing, has always been the natural cycle of life for me. Who I was held steadfast. Who I was did not bend or break, no matter what circumstances life threw my way. Because I was never built on absolutes—only adjustments.

A Quiet Reflection: Both the highs and lows shaped me into the man I am today. Looking back, those few years riding the high and then losing everything are just a small chapter in the 75 years I've had the privilege to live.

When setbacks come, I don't dwell—I get back up and keep moving forward. That's the lesson within these pages that I share with everyone I meet. There's value in every downfall if you choose to learn from it. And believe me, the collapse of my businesses taught me more than I could have imagined.

I dusted myself off and went in search of something even greater. What I found were opportunities that wouldn't have existed had I not faced that setback.

Opportunities that I would have missed, had I not endured the trials necessary to become the man who could hold those opportunities.

This is perhaps my most simple, yet vital lesson: never, ever give up. Because you never know what's around the next bend.

For The Reader: *You can't control what happens, but you can control your responses.*

Do you stay down? Do you wallow in self-pity? Or do you continue to take steps forward—no matter how big or small they may be?

Yesterday is gone. Stop knocking at its door.

The past is closed—no retakes, no rewrites. The only power you hold is now. But if your eyes are locked on the rearview, you'll miss the road unraveling beneath your feet.

Every second spent staring backward steals from the future you could be shaping. History doesn't need your permission to stay dead. The future is all yours.

What you let shatter you is up to you. **It is a decision to stay whole amidst chaos.**

*The rate at which you pick yourself up is entirely up to you. **It is only you who can make the choice to move.***

Life happens when it does. It is your choice to remain open to it all.

Chapter Ten

The Rules of Life
I Live by

Rule #1: No One Actually Knows the Rules of Life

T he most dangerous lies I ever believed were that happiness
had a manual and that anyone who gave me their advice
actually had a rulebook for me to follow. As a young boy I
heard their "rules" uttered in voices that meant well in sermons
with strong endings and in stories stitched neatly for success.
Their advice was akin to handed down heirlooms that I could
never possess.

More wealth, less meaning. Behave or burn. Those were their
rules, not mine. That rulebook never rang true in the lessons
time had to teach me, and it didn't take long before I learned
that no one actually knew the rules of life.

When I did crash after two failed businesses that ended in an
instant due to circumstances beyond my control, I started to
see much clearer. I realized that the truth of how to navigate
life never arrived with achievement—and it surely didn't exist

in the words of others. It didn't suddenly appear to me when I was flying high, building Charter Merchants International or Caputo Trucking.

But the truth did come.

It surfaced quietly in the pauses between "success" and in my questioning of how things had gone so wrong—not buried in the climb and not shattered by the falls. Instead, truth was always just waiting there beneath the noise for when I was ready to listen.

Time became my real teacher. More honest than any finish line, time taught me that nothing is ever perfect, but that you can decide what you do with the jagged pieces.

So I took the pieces of my failed ventures and fit them into something new. I decided to step away from running my own business for a bit and take all I had learned and give it freely while working for someone else. More wealth did not create more meaning, that I knew. So I stopped chasing the promised land and instead, started noticing all that still bloomed amidst the wasteland.

Instead of dwelling on what hadn't worked, I stepped into my new role at Goldseal Riviera, a prominent ice cream company, and let life be good to me.

Rule #2: Stop Looking for a Destination

The chase, the constant hustle of running my own business—of fending entirely for myself—wore me out. It wasn't because I was lost, but because I kept pretending there was somewhere concrete for me to arrive. Maps made sense when I was young—in the form of goals, benchmarks, and mile markers. But I couldn't keep chasing success at the same pace. I couldn't keep moving the goalpost further down the line every time I tried something new.

So I slowed down, worked for someone else, and learned that the joy isn't in the arrival, but in how you readjust and in how you enjoy the journey.

I answered an ad in the local newspaper where Goldseal Riviera was looking for a general manager to oversee 160 employees. The company was run by three old men, Abe and his two younger brothers, who were all approaching retirement and wanted someone to run things for them. It impressed them that I grew three businesses from the ground up, and they decided to give me a shot.

Anytime somebody gives me a shot, I'm going to do the best I can. That's what I did.

Yes, this job was a detour—a step off the path I envisioned for myself. But if there is a destination, maybe it's just where you catch your breath. This job is where I did just that. I eased my foot off the accelerator and found meaning in the journey.

Because this is how I showed up every day, output at the company increased as the employees who worked under me felt my joy. A union shop, they still felt respected, well-treated, and seen. I didn't care who you were or where you came from; every employee was important to me, and I made sure they knew it.

A few years in, I had ideas, lots of ideas, on how to grow the company even more. I approached the three bosses with a proposition: "Listen, you sell your ice cream to smaller places all over Brooklyn, New York, and Queens, but you're not in supermarkets. Supermarkets are growing, and I can get you in."

I made them a deal. "If I can grow your business revenue by $2 million, will you give me a piece of it?"

They trusted me, and their answer came easily: "Sure, Bill. We'd love to see what you can do for us."

"How about 10% of the added profits?" I asked. "Should we draw up some kind of contract?"

"No, no. We'll just shake on it. Don't worry; our word means everything."

My naivety got the best of me here; I believed them, and I shook on it. Three years later, I had a company car and a $35,000 raise in hand and had grown their business up to $11 million. When I finally went to cash in on our handshake deal to get my 10% share of the added profits—$1.1 million—the three old men reneged. The brothers simply decided they were not going to do it, and the only card I had to play was to leave.

I knew my worth, and I refused to stay in a place where I wasn't valued. I didn't hesitate. The next day, I strode into Abe's office and shook his hand. "I'm giving you my resignation," I said. "I'm leaving. How long do you need? I can give you two weeks, or I can leave today."

I was not leaving to seek some unknown destination, but instead, to walk a new path and trust in wherever it would lead me next.

Rule #3: Wealth Can't Buy Direction

Although I built that company up to $11 million, the success of it didn't give me a compass. It didn't tell me where to go or how to live. It was only when they reneged on our handshake deal that I realized comfort isn't the same as clarity. I was comfortable at Goldseal, yes, but the direction I was uniquely meant to go in life couldn't be bought.

It could only be uncovered by leaving.

So, I left—not with bitterness, but with belief that my compass still worked. I believed that the next chapter wouldn't be written by contracts or comfort, but by conviction because the rules I live by aren't carved in stone—they're shaped by motion.

I knew that my next step wasn't at that company, at least not anymore. I held unfettered confidence in myself that I would find my direction—if only I were bold enough to step away from what wasn't serving me to allow something better to come in.

To make my departure all the more sweet, my time at Goldseal Riviera ended around the same time my marriage to Milissa began. Life and time have a funny way of working like that. I walked away from business, yet I was blissfully in love with life. Both existed for me at the same moment. The truth of what I wanted most—*her*—hit me with the force of a truck. I could figure everything else out, as long as I had her by my side.

To be clear, it's not that she didn't question my choice to give up a job I was thriving in with no backup plan. But she did trust me. And I trusted the internal compass I built up after 37 years of navigating the world I was born into—and the one I created for myself.

That compass told me to walk away. So I stepped off the path and didn't look back.

I worked two more days for the three old men, so they could get things in order for my departure. Then I left Goldseal Riviera not with a lump in my throat, but with freedom in my stride.

Word quickly got out about my leaving Goldseal Riviera. I had quite the reputation in the desserts industry; my role in growing the company by $11 million was well-known. On the eve of the second day after I handed in my notice, I left the office one final time. On my way home, I was approached by Tim Metzger, the son of the CEO and owner of Dannon Yogurt. Tim introduced himself and then got straight to the point.

He was recently hired by the billionaire Leonard Kay, who owned 25 businesses around the world and counting. Tim was set to open up a brand-new desserts business with Leonard's backing, and they heard I recently became available. "Kay and I would like you to come work for us," Metzger said easily, confident in his offer. "We'd like to bring you on as vice president of manufacturing."

Truly, it happened as swiftly and seamlessly as that. My choice to honor my value as a businessman and step away when my worth wasn't appreciated opened the door to an opportunity that took me on the ride of my life.

We opened up a small factory in Brooklyn and called the business Sweet Victory. We made all kinds of sweets, but soon became well-known for our low-calorie desserts. Tim hired two food scientists to help me come up with a way to make delicious ice cream, just like the ice cream I made at Goldseal Riviera, but low-calorie and with the same great taste.

When that was a success, we expanded—low-calorie potato chips, jelly beans, popcorn, sherbert….

Soon, we were doing well enough that he opened up two stores right in the heart of Manhattan.

I created an ice cream dessert called Trufflets, a square piece of ice cream that had chocolate-covered krispies of rice nestled inside. The entire thing was coated in Belgian chocolate and covered with eclair flakes. There were 24 per box, and we started selling them in every supermarket in NYC.

They were such a hit, and the company was doing so well, that we decided to bring Sweet Victory public. We made a public offering and an initial public offering. We opened at $11.50 a share and went up to $29 a share. Along with my hefty salary, I also bought in with a high percentage of stock.

I was set.

Next, Tim sent me out to Clovis, New Mexico with two engineers. He bought an old meat plant that was fully equipped with the refrigeration we needed. Everything else we built from scratch. I told the engineers exactly what I wanted, and they figured out how to make it happen. Soon we had a machine, a system, that could make our Trufflets by the millions. The cube of ice cream was dipped into liquid nitrogen, then frozen at 320 degrees. Next, it was enrobed in Belgian chocolate and dipped into the liquid nitrogen again. The machine counted 24 bars and put them in a small box, sealed that box with plastic, put 24 boxes into a case, and put the case onto a pallet. Then it wrapped the pallet that was now ready to be shipped out. It was seamless, and it only took two people to run the entire process.

The next thing I knew, we were going national, and thanks to my work, our production system could handle it. That's when Leonard Kay began sending me and Tim on grand adventures to help publicize the business, make connections, and be seen.

First, he sent me to the Waldorf Astoria to represent Sweet Victory as a judge in a beauty contest. Then, in 1986, he sent us to Governors Island in the New York Harbor for the Liberty Weekend Opening Ceremonies. The event welcomed dignitaries, including the French President François Mitterrand and Ronald Reagan himself—who was to be the official saluter of the ships sailing into the harbor.

I celebrated with dignitaries and billionaires and shook President Reagan's hand as fireworks arced over the harbor. If I could have told the young boy I was at 7, where he would be at 37, he wouldn't believe me. Or maybe he would, since I don't remember a time when the pull towards greatness didn't tether me to the next big thing.

Milissa and I were married during my time at Sweet Victory. I met and became good friends with the owner of Frozefruit, who made ice pops on a stick with real fruit inside. His son sold rare gems, and I bought a raw diamond from him to design Milissa's ring. We got to travel the world as a young couple and lived well. We were set for life. It felt like everything that had come before this was born from the struggle to make myself into something. I found some success and made some money, but I didn't have a future that looked as bright and shiny as this one. It was the highest I'd ever been.

Until, in the blink of an eye, it was all over.

Leonard Kay, the billionaire who started Sweet Victory and provided all financial backing, passed away. Everything he owned went to his wife when he died. Instead of taking his numerous businesses and hiring managers to run them for her, she dissolved every single company he owned around the world.

That included Sweet Victory.

Almost overnight, the company shut down. I went from being vice president of a business run by a billionaire to losing it all in the blink of an eye. I lost millions of dollars in stock, my job, the factory out in New Mexico, and my big, beautiful office in Manhattan overlooking 55th and 3rd—all of it. The peak of all we'd built was suddenly just a blip on the tapestry of my life.

From riches to rags—it happened all over again.

Charter Merchants International. Caputo Trucking. Sweet Victory. In harsh succession, one after another failed. I climbed and climbed and climbed and then was forced to watch as each one slipped through my fingers. It was all sudden and unbelievable, but also, just the facts (JTF's).

Everything to nothing, everything to nothing, everything to nothing—it became an all too familiar cycle of my life.

It made me realize that nothing about the journey is within our control. But also, we still have to find kernels of truth and wisdom in it anyway. Working for a billionaire should have been the safest job I ever held. And yet, just like working for myself, it all disappeared in a split second.

I do not say this to instill fear, but to encourage freedom. If financial comfort isn't the same as clarity, it means that what we truly *need* can't be bought.

What we truly need can only be uncovered by living.

Rule #4: Contentment is a Skill, Not a Prize

I had three instances now that taught me that I would not always find peace with success. Because success is fleeting. Success is subjective. Success is in the eye of the beholder. You don't simply find peace when you get to where you're going. Instead, you must learn how to practice it.

After Sweet Victory disappeared before my eyes, I changed course. I started practicing. Instead of striving for greatness, I looked for something else. And I found it in my family—in my wife, Milissa, and in our daughter, Natalie.

Contentment snuck in when I stopped reaching and started noticing. I noticed that happiness is not a reward as we were taught to think, but instead, a habit—one you build by being present and by learning to befriend uncertainty. After I picked myself up from the crash of Sweet Victory, I decided that uncertainty and I were friends, not enemies.

There was still so much joy to be had in the simple fact that, although a business might have ended, I was still here, still evolving. I could be whatever I wanted to be. And I wanted to be a father. Fatherhood wasn't a role, it was a rhythm—one I hadn't known I was missing until she arrived.

Fatherhood is where I found meaning. It never waited for me in the hustle, like I thought it did. It waited in this, in her— *Natalie.*

Natalie came barreling into this world on December 31, 1993. I was in the room when she burst forth, screaming with a heart full of fire. The very first thing she did was turn her head and look straight at me. I'll never forget that moment. *Ever.* I was the first human being she saw, if those little eyes, brand-new to the world, could even make out the shape of my face, my smile, my joy.

But I'm sure they did.

Holding her in my arms, the first thing I did was sing to her. There was recognition there, a joy of her own as if she remembered all the music Milissa and I would play while she was pregnant. Headphones were splayed across Milissa's round belly, playing a mix of both her music and mine.

Natalie was a New Year's Eve baby. Until about the age of 6, she thought that everyone came to Times Square not to ring in the new year, but to celebrate her birthday. Every holiday, my mother-in-law would host the grandest party, and we would watch the ball drop on her 85-inch TV. Counting down the new year and singing happy birthday went hand in hand. It was the greatest celebration for a small child.

As Natalie grew, I watched her turn into an extremely bright and creative young woman—a wild horse who challenged the truths of this world even more than I did.

When she was 9, I was hitting some golf balls at the neighborhood driving range, just for fun, as I hadn't yet discovered all golf had to teach me. "Daddy, can I do that?" she asked, as she watched me hit ball after ball.

"Sure, let me go see if they have a club for you."

I got her settled in, lined up the golf ball, showed her how to hold the club, and watched as she took her first swing. Up and up the ball arced across the green. "How long has she been taking lessons?" a golf pro who was hitting his own balls next to us asked.

"Oh, I don't know, about three seconds," I replied with a grin on my face.

"You have a natural right there." He said, pointing to Natalie, who was lining up her next ball. "She's a natural."

From that day forward, Natalie started taking lessons with the pro. She joined the junior PGA and came in second in the first two tournaments she ever played. I used to chaperone her for every lesson, every tournament. Perhaps it was Natalie who unlocked my true love for golf. Perhaps she is the reason I play so much to this day and find such quiet peace whenever I stroll onto the green.

As she got older, she continued to flourish in the sport. Hofstra University eyed her for their team, and there were whispers that she was going to get a full college scholarship.

One day, Natalie walked straight up to me with conviction in her eyes, "Dad, do you mind if I quit golf?"

I didn't hesitate. "Of course. But can I ask, why do you want to quit golf?"

"I'm taking acting lessons, singing lessons, piano lessons, and navigating high school. It's just too much for me." With that, she was done. I didn't have to understand it. It was her life to live. She didn't need to find the same meaning in that tiny golf ball that I did.

Two months later, Milissa asked me if I knew why Natalie quit golf. I gave her the same reasoning that Natalie gave me.

"No, that's not the reason," Milssa knowingly replied.

"What's the reason then?" I asked, trusting she was leading me somewhere.

"You were too hard on her."

"What are you talking about? The only thing I ever said was the exact same things the coach said."

"Yeah, but you're daddy."

That sentence rewrote my rulebook, not with shame—but with clarity. Meaning slammed into me. Her path was hers alone to walk. It was not mine. My only responsibility was to guide her to trust her own instincts and internal compass, to ask better questions, and most importantly, to never be afraid of reinvention.

A Quiet Reflection: That one sentence, "Yeah, but you're daddy," taught me a big, big lesson. Truthfully, it made me change the way I was raising my daughter.

And when Natalie came home a few years later with a tattoo, a nose piercing, and colored hair, it was a lesson I learned all over again—let her make her own choices.

"Dad," she said to me, "on your deathbed, how important is this red streak in my hair gonna be?"

Wow!

This lesson has stayed with me from the moment I first heard the words because each and every one of us has our own path. Natalie has her own. Millissa has hers. And I have mine.

It doesn't mean that sometimes we don't walk together. It means that it is not up to me to control the narrative of others. It is not up to anyone but ourselves to dictate the path we walk upon in this life.

For The Reader: It is your own internal compass that you must learn to finely tune—that you must learn how to listen to. If that compass is broken, you can make it whole again. I promise.

I've seen it done. I did it.

Sometimes, you have to leap and trust the direction you're going, even if it makes no sense to others. This is how you bring more harmony into your life and less resistance.

I'll close this thought with two truths about fatherhood, golf, and life:

1. *The harder you try to control the ball, the less it listens.* **People, plans, kids—same rules apply.**

2. *The talent isn't in the club—it's in the hands that swing it.* **Tools matter less than tenacity.**

So, swing gently. Walk beside others. And remember—contentment isn't something you earn. It's something you choose.

What it is, is What it is

A big mistake I made was thinking that success was a destination—that if I could just get there, I'd be satisfied. Now I know—it's a rhythm. Now I know that there's a cadence to the bittersweet moments after the falls when you get back up and take the next step.

Some days, I walked forward. Some days, I fell back. But every step left a footprint, and every crack let the light in.

Most of the moments that changed me, that healed me, weren't spotlighted. They were simple, small. They happened when no one was looking. It wasn't the promotions, the businesses, the applause, or the big decisions. It was a quiet morning with my family. The half-conversations with a wise stranger. The solitary moments with just myself—letting my mind think and create. Those were the heartbeats that left the most impact.

When I was younger, I used to think those in-between moments were distractions. Now, at 75, I see clearly that they were the *direction* all along because life didn't care about my agenda. It had other plans for me. And the more I tried to control it, the more it taught me to let go.

It may have other plans for you, too.

This book lays forth some of my most obvious milestones, yes. But it is in the space between those milestones, in the quiet reflections at the end of each chapter, where the truth lies. For life blooms, not in the main plot, but in the space in between.

Just like my own story, you, too, are unfinished. You, too, have so many more steps to take, and you get to choose the direction. Do you walk along the path that was set out for you, or do you stray? Do you follow your own compass or someone else's? Do you take the less-traveled path? Do you follow your joy?

No matter where you go, I hope you are creative, curious, and unafraid to question what you assume you know. If something within these pages stirred you, it means I've done my job. Because I didn't write this book to give you answers. I wrote it to show you how to ask better questions.

This conclusion is not an ending, but a pause. For I have many more stories to tell

and wisdom to share.

Until next time, remember this—

Reinvention is not a single act. It is in the choices you make each day. It is in every breath, every word. I reinvented myself countless times, and I'll do it again if life calls me to. I wish the same for you. Choose a different story, one that doesn't ask for permission to be lived. Because the stories that change us aren't the ones we're handed. They're the ones we dare to write.

Those stories are where the happiness, joy, and peace you seek are found.

The next chapter isn't written here. It's waiting in you.

What it is, is what it is.

–Bill

Billisms

A collection of my simple rules for living with purpose and joy. I hope you come back to these whenever you're being challenged with redirection. Hold them near as you reinvent yourself as many times as life calls you to.

1. Never say "can't."
2. Always try your hardest.
3. Always do your best.
4. Always be proud of your effort.
5. You're stronger than you think.
6. Everyone has gifts—not the same ones. Use yours fully.
7. When you treat the world with love, it gives that love right back.
8. Always be present in the moment.
9. Never give up.
10. Find space for fun.
11. Memories may linger—but time moves forward. So should you.
12. Every life deserves kindness. Every soul, respect. Every heart, compassion.
13. Be kind. Be respectful. Be compassionate—to all things that breathe.
14. A hug is a quiet gift—you give one, and you always get one back.

15. The best days in your life have yet to happen.
16. Today is absolutely the first day of the rest of your life.
17. If you can't afford to give, give a big smile—it's free and gives plenty.
18. If you can't be kind, walk away.
19. Perspective isn't just a lens. It's a lifeline.
20. You can't control what happened, but you can control your responses.
21. Bring more harmony into your life with less resistance.
22. Never borrow trouble; it doesn't need your help.
23. Ask better questions today than you did yesterday.
24. Reinvention isn't an act; it's an atmosphere.
25. What it is, is what it is.

These aren't rules to follow. They're reminders to return to. Because what it is… is what it is.

End Note

I've walked through storms, silence, and second chances. I've seen kindness weaponized and diversity dismissed, but I've also seen it resurrected—in quiet gestures, in cracked voices, in the resilience of those who refused to turn bitter. I don't know what waits beyond this life. But I had a dream once, and dreams don't follow rules (that's what makes them beautiful).

In my dream, I was walking toward the pearly gates. There was no choir, no thunder. Just a sign. It read:

"I created kindness and diversity for a reason. If you challenged it, turn around."

I'm not done. I'm just letting you breathe. —*Bill*

++

JTF's

Acknowledgements

This first book will not be my last. But before I take another step, I need to pause and thank those who helped me find the words—and the courage—to put this one on the page.

Jessica, you stirred both memory and meaning. I couldn't have written this without your presence, your patience, and your belief in what this could become.

Tina, thank you for your intuitive guidance, steady direction, and unwavering support.

To the team who helped shape the structure and sharpen the edges, thank you for walking with me through the fog and helping me carve clarity from chaos.

To my family, thank you for being the quiet foundation beneath every chapter. Your love is the life I continue to live and write about.

To everyone I've crossed paths with, whether for a moment or a season, thank you. Your presence, however brief or lasting, has shaped the contours of this journey. May your steps be guided by truth, and may your path—however winding—lead you to the clarity and courage you were always meant to find.

And to you, the reader: if you've made it this far, you've walked beside me. Thank you for staying. I hope something here stays with you.

I wouldn't change a thing. I'd live it all again, just the way it was.

About The Author

From a childhood of poverty in Brooklyn to the battlefields of Vietnam, and ultimately to the hard-won triumphs of family and career, William's life has been anything but simple. His journey is not about perfection or privilege—it is about resilience, persistence, and the unshakable will to keep moving forward when everything says stop.

With candor and hard-earned wisdom, *The Compass Broke, I Kept Walking* reveals what it takes to turn setbacks into stepping stones. Through love, loss, and unexpected lessons found in unlikely places—even on the golf course—William shares how he built a life defined not by circumstance, but by courage and conviction.

For anyone who has struggled, questioned their direction, or wondered how to begin again, this memoir is a reminder: the path from poverty to success is not marked on any map—it's forged step-by-step, by refusing to give up.

(Written by Bill's daughter, Natalie.)